"My world collided with [barcode obscures text]
an evangelism class at W[...] had a way of inviting us all into sharing good news in a historically grounded yet imaginative way for our times. She is honest about our current realities in the Western church, yet she remains almost whimsical to the ways that Jesus can transcend it all and change the human heart."

—**Joanna la Fleur**, marketing and communications director, Alpha Canada

"With *A New and Ancient Evangelism*, Paulsen succeeds in what feels like the near-impossible task of making evangelism seem less scary and off-putting. With her gentle urging, evangelism sounds almost joyful. Sharing faith feels doable and may even be an appealing prospect after reading this warm and engaging book. Paulsen's refreshing reexamination of the conversion stories in Scripture helps guide the reader to trust their own instincts and experience to more naturally share their faith in God. The 'Experiments for Your Church to Try' section that ends the book will help readers put their new confidence to work immediately."

—**Karen Stiller**, author of *Holiness Here: Searching for God in the Ordinary Events of Everyday Life* and *The Minister's Wife: A Memoir of Faith, Doubt, Friendship, Loneliness, Forgiveness, and More*

"If truth be told, the majority of Christians in the West are not sharing their faith with anyone. We are in sore need of a fresh examination of evangelism. Paulsen's *A New and Ancient Evangelism* is that foundational text. No stone is left unturned, no pathway is ignored, as she walks us patiently through the conversion stories of Scripture to a new imagination for what evangelism can be in the post-Christendom worlds of the West. Comprehensive, engaging, profoundly theological. Read Paulsen's book and become awakened to what God is doing all around you in bringing the world to himself."

—**David Fitch**, Northern Seminary, Chicago; author of *Faithful Presence*

"Paulsen reignites our passion for evangelism. By showing that the conversion stories of the Bible offer a relational model for sharing the good news, *A New and Ancient Evangelism* invites Christians to freely participate in God's redemptive work by investing in respectful and compassionate relationships. Drawing on years of experience, Paulsen provides practical experiments of hospitality as a refreshing reminder that the triune God still cares deeply for the world and continues to transform."

—**Marilyn Draper**, Tyndale Seminary

"I'm one of those people Paulsen identifies at the beginning of this wonderful book: not interested in a book on evangelism. But I read on and was amazingly rewarded. This is a book of stories and encounters. It's about the stories of people encountering Jesus in many different ways. Paulsen helps us see the relational power of God at work through everyday circumstances and ordinary people. She invites us into reflective spaces around how we can join with Jesus in calling others to life. This is a book on evangelism I am more than happy to recommend."

—**Alan James Roxburgh**, The Missional Network

"Many Christians in the West struggle to articulate their faith with sensitivity and integrity in a pluralistic and secular world. Paulsen draws on her many years of teaching evangelism to offer a thoughtful and theological approach that equips people for witness, using stories of conversion from Scripture. Paulsen's work is a gift to those in both the church and the academy, helping to recover the e-word for our liturgical lexicon, while clarifying the role of human and divine agency in the triune God's active, saving, transforming presence in the world."

—**Ross A. Lockhart**, Vancouver School of Theology

A New and
Ancient Evangelism

A New and Ancient Evangelism

REDISCOVERING THE WAYS GOD CALLS AND SENDS

Judith Paulsen

Baker Academic
a division of Baker Publishing Group
Grand Rapids, Michigan

Published by Baker Academic
a division of Baker Publishing Group
Grand Rapids, Michigan
BakerAcademic.com

Printed in the United States of America

Library of Congress Cataloging-in-Publication Data
Names: Paulsen, Judith, 1957– author.
Title: A new and ancient evangelism : rediscovering the ways God calls and sends / Judith Paulsen.
Description: Grand Rapids, Michigan : Baker Academic, a division of Baker Publishing Group, [2024] | Includes bibliographical references and index.
Identifiers: LCCN 2023053551 | ISBN 9781540967060 (paperback) | ISBN 9781540967800 (casebound) | ISBN 9781493446209 (ebook) | ISBN 9781493446216 (pdf)
Subjects: LCSH: Evangelistic work—Biblical teaching. | Conversion—Christianity.
Classification: LCC BS2545.E82 P38 2024 | DDC 269/.2—dc23/eng/20231228
LC record available at https://lccn.loc.gov/2023053551

Cover design by Laura Klynstra
Illustrations by Carla Fern Designs via Creative Market

Baker Publishing Group publications use paper produced from sustainable forestry practices and postconsumer waste whenever possible.

24   25   26   27   28   29   30   7   6   5   4   3   2   1

Dedicated in memory of
Joan Charlotte Margetts and Eldon Stanley Davis,
missionary Methodist nurse and missionary Anglican priest,
who by word and deed introduced me to Jesus.

CONTENTS

ACKNOWLEDGMENTS

Many people encouraged and supported me in the writing of this book, but there are a few individuals who deserve particular acknowledgment. First, I want to thank Harold Percy and John Bowen, colleagues who preceded me as professors of evangelism at Wycliffe College and who first sparked my interest in the study and teaching of evangelism.

Crucial to this project coming to completion also were those who read parts of the initial manuscript and graciously took time out of their busy lives as scholars to write in support of it and offer comment on it. These include Ed Stetzer, David Fitch, Ross Lockhart, Marilyn Draper, Karen Stiller, Joanna LaFleur, and Alan Roxburgh. I will always be indebted to you for taking an interest in my work.

Two others who played a key role in the book coming to publication were David Bratt and Laura Bardolph Hubers at BBH Literary. Their expertise in fine-tuning the proposal and representing the book to various publishing houses made all the difference in me believing that this was a worthwhile project. I cannot express how much your encouragement and enthusiasm have meant to me, and I am grateful to Fleming Rutledge for putting me in touch with you.

I also want to thank the team at Baker Academic who offered their skills in design, marketing, and editing to give the book its final shape. I'm especially grateful to Eric Salo, who worked tirelessly on the copyediting. I have learned so much from your work.

Finally, I want to express my deep appreciation to Pat, my husband, who read the entire first draft of the manuscript as it was being written and offered invaluable comments and endless encouragement. Thank you. I love you.

INTRODUCTION

I teach at Wycliffe College, a grand old theological institution situated in the heart of Toronto, where we prepare students from over forty denominations to serve as Christian leaders.[1] One of the distinctives of our master of divinity degree is that for several decades it has included a required course in evangelism. Several years ago, I realized that as the instructor of this course I needed to grapple with two key problems. First, most students entering the class held a negative view of evangelism, but they hadn't acknowledged it or reflected on why this was the case. Second, they viewed evangelism as a daunting task of the church but had little understanding of how evangelism connected to theology or to biblical texts (other than perhaps the Great Commission[2]).

Could I find a way to help them reflect on their negative biases against evangelism and cultivate in them a healthier, God-centered

---

1. Wycliffe College is an evangelical graduate school of theology, rooted in the Anglican tradition, that has trained church leaders from across North America and around the world. It was founded in 1879 and is one of seven theological colleges that make up the Toronto School of Theology at the University of Toronto.

2. Matthew 28:18–20: "And Jesus came and said to them, 'All authority in heaven and on earth has been given to me. Go therefore and make disciples of all nations, baptizing them in the name of the Father and of the Son and of the Holy Spirit and teaching them to obey everything that I have commanded you. And remember, I am with you always, to the end of the age.'"

view of mission? Might the conversion stories of Scripture hold the key to instilling a quiet confidence in sharing the faith and in helping others do the same, while also grounding their preaching, teaching, and leadership skills in God's own activity as revealed in Scripture? And perhaps most importantly, could these stories help these future church leaders cultivate churches that better shared the faith with a world deeply in need of the gospel?

I am more convinced than ever that the conversion stories of Scripture must shape our understanding of how conversion takes place, which in turn will dramatically change our practice of evangelism. By exploring and reflecting on the stories of transformation in the lives of a powerful general, a blind beggar, a royal treasurer, four fishermen, a God-fearing outsider, a fearful jailer, a religious scholar, a wealthy businesswoman, and a Hebrew altar boy, the church can hear afresh an ancient calling to something richer than the attitudes and approaches to evangelism that have proved so fruitless.

For several years Wycliffe's evangelism course has started its first class session with two short exercises. First, as students enter the class, they see a desk with two stacks of cards and a note which simply says, "Greetings! Choose a card." One stack contains cards bearing the word "evangelist," while the other stack contains cards bearing the made-up word "evangelee." Year after year an overwhelming majority of students pick up a card from this second stack with the made-up word.

When I ask students why they chose the evangelee card, they often report that they thought I might make them do a role-play exercise in which they had to be an evangelist, and they wanted to avoid that. Others admitted not knowing what "evangelee" meant, but it had to be better than being an evangelist. Every year these students, training to be leaders in the church, reveal a negative bias against the word "evangelist."

The second exercise in that first class involves a game of word association. After naming several random nouns, I throw out the word "evangelist." The responses are instructive. Upon hearing the word, many students have said "Billy Graham," but responses have also included "television," "crusade," "Mormons," "street preacher," and, interestingly, "used car salesman." Perhaps the most fascinating response came when a student, who had been happily replying to previous words, suddenly drew a blank. When I asked her what had happened in that moment, she replied, "My stomach just kind of tightened up."

At the very least, these simple interactive exercises demonstrate something surprising in people training for ordained and lay leadership in the church: very few of them like the word "evangelist," and they certainly don't think of themselves as one. Such negative feelings certainly seem to be widespread in the church, based on the activities and teaching focus of churches. Most churches seem to be avoiding the teaching or practice of evangelism, and apparently this has been the case for quite some time.

A survey of 262 churches within the Disciples of Christ denomination, conducted almost two decades ago, examined what 25,000 members said about their home church. Participants were asked to rank 53 statements in terms of level of agreement.[3] The statement ranked last was "This congregation provides training in sharing Christ with others." The statement ranked second to last was "This church is effectively reaching unchurched persons."

Five years later a major research project funded by the Lilly Foundation examined statistics drawn from 30,000 churches across seven denominations in the US.[4] Apart from churches in the southern Bible Belt and churches with a specific ethnic focus, fewer than 1 percent of the churches examined were baptizing a significant number of adults (adult baptism being a strong measure of evangelism in a post-Christendom society). Out of the 30,000 churches, this study identified fewer than 150 that were consistently making

3. Christian Church (Disciples of Christ), Homeland Ministries and Church Extension Faithful Planning Congregational Survey Results, 2001–2005, cited by Reese, *Unbinding the Gospel*, 4.

4. Reese, *Unbinding the Gospel*, 30. The seven denominations were American Baptist Churches USA, Christian Church (Disciples of Christ), Evangelical Lutheran Church in America, Presbyterian Church USA, Reformed Church in America, United Church of Christ, and United Methodist Church.

new disciples.[5] Although few churches would ever state that evangelism is unimportant to them, the data on church practices suggests just that.

What about attitudes toward evangelism in broader society? A decade after the above research in churches, a public opinion poll on religion was conducted across all sectors of the Canadian population. Participants were given a list of twelve words that had some religious association and were asked to identify those words that held a positive meaning for them.[6] Of the Canadians deemed "nonbelievers" (on the basis of their practices and beliefs), 0 percent viewed the word "evangelism" positively. Of those deemed "spiritually uncertain," only 1 percent viewed the word "evangelism" positively. Of those deemed "privately faithful" (those who believed in God and prayed monthly but had no connection to a faith community), only 4 percent thought the word had a positive meaning. And perhaps most tellingly, even among those deemed to be "religiously committed" (believed in God, prayed, and participated regularly in their faith community), only 29 percent viewed "evangelism" as having a positive meaning. Among this group, only the words "karma" and "mystical" held more negative associations than the word "evangelism."[7]

What is at the root of these pervasively negative attitudes toward evangelism? What makes evangelism so distasteful to so many people? There are likely multiple factors, including images we have in our heads about what evangelism is, approaches to evangelism that we ourselves have experienced, and assumptions that we hold about what an evangelist does. Let's look at each of these factors individually, drawing on what people in churches across North America have shared with me as I've talked with them about evangelism.

5. Reese, *Unbinding the Gospel*, 30.
6. The words included "forgiveness," "morality," "mercy," "meditation," "karma," "salvation," "religion," "resurrection," "born-again," "mystical," "theology," and "evangelism."
7. "A Spectrum of Spirituality," Angus Reid Institute, April 13, 2017, p. 10, http://angusreid.org/wp-content/uploads/2017/04/2017.04.12_Faith_Wave_1_Part _1.pdf.

Images in Our Head

Often a negative bias against something is based less on factual data and more on the images that come to mind when we hear a particular word. When some people hear the word "evangelism," what comes to mind is a mechanistic exchange: "Just say these words and you're in." Though most people who are encouraging someone to pray the "sinner's prayer" likely view such a prayer as only a first step in a lifelong journey as a follower of Jesus, this sort of scripted approach has been viewed as a kind of recipe for salvation, trivializing the mystery and grace of God and reducing salvation to a magical incantation, dependent more on what we say than on what God has done in Christ.[8] Few Christians want to treat others in such a mechanistic way, but this is the image of evangelism they carry. So, they simply don't share the faith at all.

For other people, the picture of evangelism that may come to mind is an objectifying, "one more notch in my belt" image. Zealous youth leaders who take groups of teenagers out to share gospel tracts with strangers on their city streets aren't necessarily motivated by self-glory, nor do they want to encourage it among their youth. But at the end of the evening when everyone reports how many people they spoke to, how many took a tract, how many allowed them to pray with them, and how many were saved, there may well be a sense that the people they engaged with were more like sales targets than people God might mysteriously and purposefully be drawing into relationship with himself.

---

8. While there are slightly different versions of the "sinner's prayer," they all involve the person admitting their sin, asking for God's grace and forgiveness, affirming belief in the death and resurrection of Jesus, and committing to follow him as their Lord and Savior. Here is the version that one of the twentieth century's most famous evangelists, Billy Graham, invited people to pray: "Dear God, I know I am a sinner. I want to turn from my sins, and I ask for Your forgiveness. I believe that Jesus Christ is Your Son. I believe He died for my sins and that You raised Him to life. I want Him to come into my heart and to take control of my life. I want to trust Jesus as my Savior and follow Him as my Lord from this day forward. In Jesus' name, amen." "Start Your New Life with Christ," Peace with God (website), accessed October 25, 2023, https://peacewithgod.net/steps.

A third negative stereotype that some people carry about evangelism is a triumphalistic "Accept this now or you're a goner!" image. While Christians should boldly proclaim the uniqueness of Jesus Christ and the salvation found in him alone, we are also now painfully aware of the damage done by forced or coerced conversions that occurred under colonial Christianity. Such triumphalism seems to have been linked more to cultural imperialism than to the kingdom of God. That sort of evangelism leaves a bad taste in the mouth. For example, as Canadians grow in their knowledge of the horrors of the church-run residential schools, which thousands of First Nations, Métis, and Inuit children were forced to attend, they often feel shame and sorrow that the gospel was linked so closely to a colonial agenda of cultural genocide.

Finally, there are Christians who consider evangelism to be disrespectful. Particularly in the context of apologetics, it can seem that the forceful presentation of an excellent argument, rather than a lived embodiment of the gospel, has become the goal. One might call this the "only an idiot would argue with this!" image of evangelism. Those who oppose this form of evangelism see the inherent disconnect, a sort of cognitive dissonance, between the *message* of the gospel and the *method* by which the gospel is shared, and they want nothing to do with that disconnect.

Of course, Christian apologetics need not carry an attitude of disrespect, as John Stackhouse has shown in his book *Humble Apologetics*. It is possible to present a well-constructed argument for the faith without being overbearing or unkind. Nevertheless, a certain hubris has come to be associated with some of the most well-known apologists, and most Christians want nothing to do with such an attitude.

Approaches We Have Experienced

The negative images people link with the word "evangelism" are not the only hurdles Christians need to get over to better share their faith. There are also the negative *approaches* we have experienced firsthand. Some have been intrusive and impersonal, such as the doorbell rung by two well-dressed missionaries with a Book of Mormon in hand. Not many of us see ourselves going door to door to talk to people we have never met, even if we believe this is something that true evangelists do.

Or perhaps the word "evangelism" reminds us of that awkward and thoroughly nonrelational moment when a stranger on the subway thrust a flyer into our hand. Nothing in that context gives us a sense that they wanted to know us or cared about us as a person. If our experience of evangelism is limited to such an experience, how likely are we to share the faith?

Worse yet, what if our experience of evangelism is hearing someone loudly preaching at a busy intersection in our neighborhood? The power of what might essentially be a good message can so easily be obscured by the method, depending on the street preacher and how they engage with the people gathered to listen. If the person seemed angry, judgmental, condemning, or simply incoherent, this experience may deter us from seeing ourselves as witnesses for Christ.

Finally, some Christians have experienced a bait-and-switch approach to evangelism. Friendship evangelism, an approach to evangelism that was popular in the 1990s, at times fell into this category. This approach involved churches encouraging their members to make friends with a non-Christian neighbor or colleague to share the gospel with them. How could such an approach bear bad fruit? Well, the devil is in the details.

I have a close non-Christian friend whose daughter was invited to a new friend's house. She and the other mom worked together, and their daughters were the same age. When the little girl got to her new friend's house, she noticed there was a picture of her family on their fridge. The photo had been taken when the two families had gotten together for a backyard BBQ. When the little girl asked why they had the picture on the fridge, the other girl replied, "Because we're praying for your family to become Christians." When the daughter shared this information with my friend, she felt hurt and used. She had thought this new family genuinely wanted to be their friends. Now it felt like something else. And while this Christian family may have been completely authentic and loving in their motivations, imagine how they would have felt if they knew they had made my friend feel like some kind of "religious project." I doubt that even that Christian family would have been keen to join in their church's next evangelistic effort.

Assumptions about Evangelists

Interestingly, it's not only negative *images* and *experiences* that can deter Christians from sharing their faith. Sometimes this can happen as a result of a positive view of what it means to be an evangelist. In my work, both at Wycliffe College and with churches across Canada, I often ask people to tell me who they think of when they think of an evangelist. As with my students, many quickly reply, "Billy Graham!" As someone who, over many decades, held countless evangelistic events around the globe, Graham is revered by many as the quintessential evangelist: a brilliant communicator, a skilled preacher, someone with a deep knowledge of the Bible, and an anointed and strategic Christian leader. He preached the gospel to millions, who were then connected to local churches for further nurturing in the faith. In short, he was exceptionally gifted.

But how might this positive view of a brilliant evangelist negatively affect the average Christian today? Billy Graham's giftedness may actually serve as a work-avoidance tactic, as lay Christians assume they don't know the Bible well enough or won't be able to present compelling enough reasons for the faith or don't have the right sort of charismatic personality to be an evangelist. After all, how many Billy Grahams could there be in the world?

Still a Few More Factors

There are still even more reasons that Christians are deterred from sharing their faith. What else makes evangelism distasteful? One factor may be guilt applied from the pulpit: "This is your Christian duty, so why aren't you better at evangelizing?" While I believe that sharing the good news of what God has done in and through Jesus

Christ is at the center of the church's mission, making people feel guilty about not sharing the faith is great for stirring up feelings of shame, but it is a poor motivator for changing behavior. It is more likely to cause Christians to search for the reason why *they are not suited* for the job.

Coming to the rescue of Christians who already feel negatively about evangelism is what might be the most magnificent biblical evangelism escape clause ever. In the letter to the Ephesians we read, "He himself granted that some are apostles, prophets, evangelists, pastors and teachers" (4:11). That little word "some" indicates, after all, that to be an evangelist may simply not be *everyone's* responsibility, right? "And thank God for that!" timid Christians whisper under their breath.

Another factor that may be deterring Christians across the West from sharing the faith is the pervasive narrative, both inside and outside the church, of the secularization of the West. While it's true that church attendance is down across most denominations in North America and Europe today, research indicates that this narrative of pervasive secularization may be overstated. True, people may have stopped (or not started) going to church, but they have not stopped having spiritual questions, longings, and experiences. While there is an increasing number of those who do not belong to any religious tradition, many of these people nonetheless classify themselves as "spiritual but not religious."[9] They have rejected formalized religion but not spirituality altogether.

Although Canada is publicly a secular society, a majority of Canadians fall into the personal categories of "privately faithful" or "spiritually uncertain," with only 19 percent of the population falling into the "nonbeliever" category.[10] The United States also shows this same contrast between church attendance and religious significance, as seen in recent research conducted by the Pew Research Center. While only 25 percent of the American population

9. Mercadante, *Belief without Borders*, 4.
10. Ray Pennings and Jenisa Los, "The Shifting Landscape of Faith in Canada," Cardus, 2022, p. 13, https://www.cardus.ca/research/spirited-citizenship/reports/the-shifting-landscape-of-faith-in-canada.

attend church weekly, 40 percent consider religion "very important" in their lives.[11] This difference suggests that plenty of Americans have spiritual beliefs, questions, and longings. In short, the narrative of the secularization of the West must not be used as a reason to give up on sharing the gospel. Rather, this narrative should be seen for what it is: another work-avoidance tactic that Christians are happy to use to avoid something they view negatively.

Finally, we note one last reason Christians across the West may not be sharing the gospel, and it is perhaps the most troubling. In addition to their negative images, experiences, and assumptions about evangelism, they may have lost confidence that Jesus really is the Bread of Life, the Good Shepherd, and the Way, the Truth, and the Life (John 6:35; 10:14; 14:6). If this is the case, the church in the West will again need to be renewed through a fresh outpouring of the Holy Spirit, a deeper practice of prayer, a reacquaintance with the story of Scripture, and the teaching and preaching of who Christ is and what God has accomplished in his birth, life, death, and resurrection. New Christians are often the best witnesses to Christ, principally because they have a compelling sense of the person and work of Jesus in their own life. Until more of the Western church rediscovers this truth, hesitancy among many Christians to share their faith will likely continue.

Finding a New Way Forward

We've seen that the interaction of many different factors has given rise to an array of negative attitudes toward evangelism among Christians. However, the data profiling the sharp decline in church attendance across North America, together with data on Christians' own attitudes toward evangelism, makes at least one thing clear: more than just their *attitudes* are being affected. The major-

11. Gregory A. Smith, "About Three-in-Ten U.S. Adults Are Now Religiously Unaffiliated," Pew Research Center, December 14, 2021, pp. 5–6, https://www .pewresearch.org/religion/2021/12/14/about-three-in-ten-u-s-adults-are-now -religiously-unaffiliated.

ity of Christians in North America are simply not sharing their faith with anyone. How might the church replace this aversion to evangelism with a renewed love for sharing the good news of Jesus Christ?

Sharing Faith, by Thomas Groome, a leading scholar in Christian pedagogy, has become a foundational text exploring how Christian faith is cultivated and transmitted. Groome suggests that for new learning to occur for someone coming to faith, five movements must happen in that person's life: (1) naming or expressing their present practice, (2) critical reflection on that practice, (3) having the Christian story and vision made accessible to them, (4) appropriating the Christian story to their own story, and (5) making a decision or response for lived Christian faith.[12] If these five movements are the path of learning for someone coming to faith, perhaps they are also a clue to how the church can learn new and yet ancient truths about how that journey occurs. And perhaps those truths can help the church learn afresh how to share the faith today.

In this book, I connect these five steps to the church being sent out into the world with the message of what God has done and is doing in Jesus Christ. I have already named the church's present evangelistic practice (or lack thereof) and began reflecting on this as the key adaptive challenge facing the twenty-first-century church. But it is Groome's third and fourth movements that are my primary focus in this book: delving deeply into the conversion stories of Scripture so that the church in the West can again learn ancient wisdom about how God draws people to himself and how, empowered by the Holy Spirit, we as the people of God can be his instruments in that great venture.

These conversion stories from Scripture embody an ancient, respectful, and relational model of evangelism, one that understands evangelism to be initiated by God, empowered by the Holy Spirit, and Christocentric in focus. Each story offers lessons that point first to who God is, how he is at work in the world, and how he

12. Groome, *Sharing Faith*, 146–48.

calls people to himself. Each points to how the Holy Spirit guides, directs, and empowers God's people to share the good news with those he is already at work in. Each story disarms common assumptions about how the human heart is turned toward God. My hope is that this book will point the church to healthier practices of evangelism, both as individuals and as communities of faith in our time, for the sake of the world God loves.

DISCUSSION QUESTIONS

1. When you hear the word "evangelist," what first comes to mind?
2. Do you see yourself as an evangelist? Why or why not?
3. Share with the group who first shared the gospel with you.
4. Have you ever had an opportunity to share your faith in Christ with someone? If so, what did that look like and what was the response?

The Conversion of Someone Who Had Never Seen

As he walked along, he saw a man blind from birth. His disciples asked him, "Rabbi, who sinned, this man or his parents, that he was born blind?" Jesus answered, "Neither this man nor his parents sinned; he was born blind so that God's works might be revealed in him. We must work the works of him who sent me while it is day; night is coming, when no one can work. As long as I am in the world, I am the light of the world." When he had said this, he spat on the ground and made mud with the saliva and spread the mud on the man's eyes, saying to him, "Go, wash in the pool of Siloam" (which means Sent). Then he went and washed and came back able to see. The neighbors and those who had seen him before as a beggar began to ask, "Is this not the man who used to sit and beg?" Some were saying, "It is he." Others were saying, "No, but it is someone like him." He kept saying, "I am he." But they kept asking him, "Then how were your eyes opened?" He answered, "The man called Jesus made mud, spread it on my eyes, and said to me, 'Go to Siloam and wash.' Then I went and washed and received my sight." They said to him, "Where is he?" He said, "I do not know."

They brought to the Pharisees the man who had formerly been blind. Now it was a Sabbath day when Jesus made the mud and opened his eyes. Then the Pharisees also began to ask him how he had received his sight. He said to them, "He put mud on my eyes. Then I washed, and now I see." Some of the Pharisees said, "This man is not from God, for he does not observe the Sabbath." Others said, "How can a man who is a sinner perform such signs?" And they were divided. So they said again to the blind man, "What do you say about him? It was your eyes he opened." He said, "He is a prophet."

The Jews did not believe that he had been blind and had received his sight until they called the parents of the man who had received his sight and asked them, "Is this your son, who you say was born blind? How then does he now see?" His parents answered, "We know that this is our son and that he was born blind, but we do not know how it is that now he sees, nor do we know who opened his eyes. Ask him; he is of age. He will speak for himself." His parents said this because they were afraid of the Jews, for the Jews had already agreed that anyone who confessed Jesus to be the Messiah would be put out of the synagogue. Therefore his parents said, "He is of age; ask him."

So for the second time they called the man who had been blind, and they said to him, "Give glory to God! We know that this man is a sinner." He answered, "I do not know whether he is a sinner. One thing I do know, that though I was blind, now I see." They said to him, "What did he do to you? How did he open your eyes?" He answered them, "I have told you already, and you would not listen. Why do you want to hear it again? Do you also want to become his disciples?" Then they reviled him, saying, "You are his disciple, but we are disciples of Moses. We know that God has spoken to Moses, but as for this man, we do not know where he comes from." The man answered, "Here is an astonishing thing! You do not know where he comes from, yet he opened my eyes. We know that God does not listen to sinners, but he does listen to one who worships him and obeys his will. Never since the world began has it been heard that anyone opened the eyes of a person born blind. If this man were not from God, he could do nothing." They answered him, "You were born entirely in sins, and are you trying to teach us?" And they drove him out.

Jesus heard that they had driven him out, and when he found him he said, "Do you believe in the Son of Man?" He answered, "And who is he, sir? Tell me, so that I may believe in him." Jesus said to him, "You have seen him, and the one speaking with you is he." He said, "Lord, I believe." And he worshiped him. Jesus said, "I came into this world for judgment, so that those who do not see may see and those who do see may become blind." Some of the Pharisees who were with him heard this and said to him, "Surely we are not blind, are we?" Jesus said to them, "If you were blind, you would not have sin. But now that you say, 'We see,' your sin remains."

—John 9:1–41

T his healing and conversion of a man born blind is one of the most memorable stories in the Gospel of John. While it begins as a simple interaction between two people, it explodes into a conflict that ripples outward, eventually affecting not just the man himself but his closest relatives, his neighbors, key religious leaders, and everyone in the local synagogue in Jerusalem. Pushback against the most powerful leaders in the faith community, and an affront to the long-standing Sabbath rules of that community, drive the action. This is a story of both pain and promise.

Before we focus on the various players involved in this story, let's first attend to the person with whom everything begins, Jesus. The story tells us that this interaction occurred "as he walked along." Jesus was on the move. When we read Scripture, it is always beneficial to read the preceding passage. Toward the end of the previous chapter, we learn that Jesus was walking away from the temple in Jerusalem, where he had engaged in a heated discussion with the religious leaders about not only his identity and authority but also theirs. Jesus claimed that his authority to teach and heal came directly from God, the One who sent him (John 8:42). The claim is repeated five times within the space of just seventeen verses in John's Gospel.

The argument culminated in Jesus making the extraordinary (and dangerous) claim that "before Abraham was, I am." Every Jew present would have recognized that, by making that statement, Jesus was claiming to be God. This claim, unsurprisingly, shocked and angered the religious leaders. The heated discussion quickly escalated into an interaction so charged with emotion that they attempted to kill Jesus. The story tells us that Jesus somehow hid himself, slipped away from the temple grounds (John 8:58), and continued walking through the crowded streets of Jerusalem.

He had engaged in debate with the religious leaders about who he was. He was now about to *demonstrate* who he was in his interaction with the man who had been born blind. But why focus on this question of Jesus's identity in a book about evangelism? Because one key truth can be discerned in every single conversion story explored in this book: conversion begins with God's own activity in a person's life. Conversion is first about who God is and what he wants to accomplish in our lives and in the life of the world.

Conversion Is First and Foremost a Work of God

It may sound obvious that conversion is about the work of God, but often the way we speak about evangelism makes it sound like evangelism is all about us. Us having the right communication skills. Us having extensive Bible knowledge or a compelling testimony or the answers to difficult philosophical questions. Us having a special gift for evangelism. Yet, in the conversion stories of Scripture we see time and again that the story begins with the living triune God's own action. In the present story we are told that God the Son saw a man blind from birth and acted on that man's behalf.

Think of some of the people around you in your everyday life: the barista who passes you your coffee, the colleague in the Zoom meeting, the person living on the streets whom you avoid looking at, the friend you meet up with after work, the new neighbor, the other parents on the sidelines of the soccer pitch. Do we think of them as people whom God is *looking* at and people whom God *sees*? Do we take time to imagine what "works" God might want to display in their lives? Above all, do we truly believe that the God who called all reality into being is calling such people into relationship with him? If we can help Christians answer yes to those questions, perhaps they'll be more confident in sharing their faith with the non-Christians in their lives. Many Christians seem to simply prefer to avoid people who don't know about Jesus. Or rather, they avoid talking to such people about God, opting instead for the status quo.

The man born blind was someone people might have wanted to avoid, for he was clearly on the margins of society with seemingly no hope or means of changing his status. As someone born blind, he would have never known what it was like to see. He wouldn't have known anything different from the life he had, in all probability the life of a beggar. There is no indication in the story that he was expecting anything different than the status quo on that day. It's likely that the best he was hoping for was a handout.

The disciples question whether his disability was caused by his own sin or that of his parents. That a disability was caused by sin was the common view at the time. But Jesus dispelled this notion and pointed instead to this happening "so that God's works might be revealed in him" (John 9:3). We might assume that this simply refers to him being given the gift of sight. But Jesus used the plural "works." One such work of God was undoubtedly the miraculous healing of his sight, but a second work, or gift, was this man's spiritual rebirth. They both began with an action of God.

God is the primary Healer and the primary Evangelist. God is on the move and sees people with real needs and longings, even those not yet recognized. He acts in order to draw people to himself. Conversion relies on God: the love of God the Father, the redemptive work of God the Son, and the convicting work of God the Holy Spirit. The conversion stories of Scripture highlight again and again that we, as apprentices of Jesus (the word "Christian" literally means "little Christ"), are invited into the marvelous work of God drawing people to himself.

Conversion Often Involves a Process

Much has been written and preached regarding this man's perception of Jesus as it progresses throughout the conversion story: The man first identified Jesus as "the *man* called Jesus" (9:11). He then shifted to the bold statement, "He is a *prophet*" (v. 17). He later prodded the religious leaders with the sarcastic question, "Do you also want to become his disciples?" (v. 27), suggesting that he already may be including himself in that category. He then argued that Jesus must be from God, because "if this man were not from God, he could do nothing" (v. 33). Finally, when Jesus went looking for the man after he was expelled by the Pharisees, he asked the man if he believed in the Son of Man. After further clarification about Jesus's identity, the formerly blind man replied, "*Lord*, I believe" and followed this affirmation with an extraordinary action; as the text notes, "He *worshiped* him" (v. 38). Step by step the man came to a fuller understanding of Jesus, culminating in worship. Throughout this journey we see the importance of this man telling his own version of what happened to him. As he told his story, his story shaped his understanding.

What does the process of conversion in this story teach us about healthy evangelism in our own context? It reminds us that we need to meet people where they are, trusting that, as we walk with them through various stages, God will bring about spiritual growth. Too often we think sharing the faith should begin with talking to people about Jesus, but there are important steps that precede this. A gardening metaphor can help us unpack this idea, as cultivating faith bears similarities to cultivating a garden.

Break Ground, Till the Soil, Remove Stones

Growing a garden requires more than tearing open a packet of seeds and scattering them on the ground. Consider the steps you might take to grow a flourishing vegetable garden. If it's totally new ground, you will need to till the soil. The heavy sod of grasses and weeds needs to be dug through and removed, then the underlying soil needs to be loosened with some kind of plow or tiller. Breaking ground is no easy or quick task. Similarly, when hoping to cultivate faith in someone, you may need to break through the ground of their prior assumptions (or ignorance or disinterest) about Christ or Christianity. This tilling often happens in the context of authentic relationship.

In their book *I Once Was Lost: What Postmodern Skeptics Taught Us about Their Path to Jesus*, Don Everts and Doug Schaupp describe the results of their research, conducted primarily on American university campuses, exploring the process of conversion. Talking with recent converts to Christianity, they discern five thresholds that are common steps in the typical journey of faith today. They describe the first threshold as moving from *distrust to trust*. The authors note the role of authentic relationship in people crossing this first threshold: "Somewhere along the line, they learned to trust a Christian."[1]

With present-day church scandals and pastoral abuses, as well as historic wrongs committed by the church in alignment with colonialism, many people today hold a deep skepticism of both the church and Christianity, and it may be very difficult to rid themselves of distrust. Using our gardening metaphor, they may well have grown a thick layer of sod that prevents the seeds of the gospel from even being planted. However, *authentic* friendships with Christians may be one of the most important tools with which God breaks through this tough ground and previously skeptical people become open to learning about what makes someone whom they have come to trust and respect follow the teachings and way of Jesus.

Once the soil has been tilled, the next step is to get rid of the stones that the tilling process stirred up. Once people have developed some level of trust in a particular Christian or group of Christians, they begin to ask questions, particularly those arising from their negative assumptions and views: If God is so good, why is there so much suffering in the world? What about all the horrific things done in the name of religion through the centuries? What is the difference between believing Santa is alive and believing Jesus is alive? Aren't Christians against science? How can the Bible, written so long ago, have any relevance today? These valid

1. Everts and Schaupp, *I Once Was Lost*, 23.

questions can be seen as rocks churned up as a result of engaging with a Christian whom they've come to trust. This stage in the conversion process is what Everts and Schaupp describe as the movement from *complacent to curious*, the second threshold.

How should Christians best respond to someone in this second stage? A variety of responses are likely going to be helpful. First, they can answer questions to the best of their ability, seeking help in answering such questions by consulting with other Christians or by giving their conversation partner some resources to explore. There is an engaging series of videos, produced by Scripture Union Ireland, called *Nua*.[2] This series addresses some common questions non-Christians are asking today and does so in a visually engaging and playful manner. This and other apologetic resources can be useful, but perhaps the most important apologetic for the Christian faith is a lived apologetic, as someone comes to see the difference that faith makes in a Christian's everyday life. There is no better apologetic for the Christian faith than Christlikeness seen in the life of a flesh-and-blood person that a non-Christian has come to know. This ought to give Christians food for thought. Their own spiritual maturity—seen in such character traits as the fruit of the Spirit (love, joy, peace, patience, kindness, goodness, faithfulness, gentleness, and self-control) and in such countercultural habits as prayer, worship, simple living, and caring for the poor—often speaks more strongly to non-Christians than does an apologetic argument for the faith. Nevertheless, such resources may still help answer key questions non-Christians have about what we believe and why we believe it. Both words and deeds are part of the tilling and rock-removal stages of pre-evangelism.

Fertilize the Soil

There is more that Christians can do at this stage as we walk with someone on the road to conversion. Beyond being a friend and

2. https://nuafilmseries.org. This series, geared specifically to teens and young adults, is now freely downloadable through this link, which also provides more information on each of the videos.

addressing their questions as best we can, we are also given two important gifts to aid us in this work of pre-evangelism: prayer and fasting. The church today often fails to see the connection between mission and these Christian practices. In prayer, we thank God for our non-Christian friend and ask the Holy Spirit to guide us in our conversations and interactions. Fasting is a powerful discipline to help us both focus on prayer and serve as a physical sacrifice offered to God on behalf of our friend. Our prayer should be that the Holy Spirit will do two things that help fertilize the soil out of which faith can grow and blossom: (1) keep us in step with whatever God is doing in that person's life, and (2) keep us faithful to the task of joining in God's work of preparing them for the next stage in the process of conversion.

Planting Seeds

While some arms of the church emphasize the witness of deeds and others emphasize the witness of words, both are necessary. The witness of deeds often precedes the witness of words, but at some point, for a person to take the step of committing to live as an apprentice of Christ, they need to hear who Christ is, why he came, what he taught, why he died and rose again, and what his lordship means in our lives today.

This primary work of evangelism can be done by simply inviting a non-Christian friend into a series of conversations centered on the Gospel accounts. This could include discussion on key events in the life of Jesus, such as his birth, his early life, the emergence of his public ministry, his key teachings, his death and resurrection, his ascension, and the commissioning of his followers. Alternatively, these conversations could discuss key interactions Jesus had with particular people, such as the Samaritan woman at the well, Zacchaeus, the Roman centurion, Nicodemus, Mary Magdalene, Peter, Judas, or Thomas. These discussions, centered on both friendship and a shared curiosity, can be incredibly fruitful for planting gospel seeds. (For some tips on how to get these conversations started, see the appendix under "Experiment #2.")

Everts and Schaupp, in their study of paths to conversion, emphasize that a third threshold people often cross on this journey is to move from *being closed to change to being open to change*.[3] In this critical step a person becomes open to something changing in themselves and in their lives. In one sense this is a tipping point because it means they are now ready to make a more intentional exploration of who Jesus might be and who he might be to them. Everts and Schaupp describe the fourth and next threshold as moving from *meandering to seeking*.[4] In this stage of the conversion process a Christian might invite their friend to a program for seekers and explorers, such as the Alpha Course,[5] Christianity Explored,[6] Jesus the Game Changer,[7] or the Being With Course.[8] These particular resources may prove useful, but many churches develop their own program to help people explore their particular questions and the teachings of the Christian faith. Churches should be well-acquainted with these tools prior to use and be ready to adapt the content for their own context.

Watering, Waiting, Thinning, and Weeding

What can Christians do as they walk with a friend during this stage of conversion? Just as a gardener must do the patient work of watering, waiting, thinning, and weeding, so too there is patient work for the Christian in this stage. We can continue to be a friend and walk with them, and we can continue to listen and

3. Everts and Schaupp, *I Once Was Lost*, 24.

4. Everts and Schaupp, *I Once Was Lost*, 24.

5. The eleven sessions of this video series are free and downloadable at https://alpha.org.

6. https://www.youtube.com/@ChristianityExplored. This seven-session, free downloadable teaching series offers an introduction to the Christian faith.

7. This film series explores how the teachings of Jesus have been foundational to the worldview of Western democracies. https://www.olivetreemedia.com.au/jesus-the-game-changer.

8. This ten-session course emphasizes the role of community in people's exploration of the faith. It invites people to discover faith in the context of discovering friendship, placing belonging before believing. https://being-with.org/being-with-one.

respond to their questions. We can accompany them to programs offered by the church. We can read and discuss a book with them. Most importantly, we can continue to pray for them, trusting that God sees them and patiently leads them as they grow in their understanding of who God is, just as Jesus did with the man born blind. Evangelism and prayer go hand in hand. The key to evangelism in this stage is to follow the Spirit's lead. We need to recognize this as a time to be patient and to celebrate the growth we see while continuing to nurture the process as it comes to fruition.

Harvesting

A harvest of ripe tomatoes, golden butternut squash, luscious Swiss chard, or raspberries always brings joy. There's something amazing about the process of cultivation, as tiny seeds yield a bounty that is gathered and brought to the gardener's dinner table. It is just the same with the process of conversion. The story of Jesus's healing of the man who was born blind typifies that what begins as a small seed (an interaction with "the man called Jesus") can grow into something life-giving and beautiful ("Lord, I believe" and "He worshiped him"). Everts and Schaupp describe this stage of conversion as the last threshold, when a person crosses "the threshold of the kingdom itself."[9]

What does this season of harvest look like on the ground? Historically, this has been the time for baptism preparation, which has included teaching on such things as the historic creeds, the Lord's Prayer, the Sermon on the Mount, and key Christian doctrines and practices. As we see in many of the conversion stories of the New Testament, this period of harvest usually culminates in the sacrament of baptism. Since the days of the early church, the person to be baptized publicly renounces the forces of evil, repents of their own sin, and turns to Jesus Christ as their Savior and Lord. As in the story of the man born blind, Christian conversion does

9. Everts and Schaupp, *I Once Was Lost*, 24.

not culminate in a person simply accepting particular religious ideas or propositions. It culminates in a person, empowered by the Holy Spirit, coming to worship the living God made known to us in Jesus Christ.

We've seen in this biblical conversion story how conversion is a process of encounter, learning, and change. But it also points to both the pain and the promise of someone coming to know and follow Jesus, as well as the inherently missional nature of conversion.

The Pain of Conversion

This story is one of healing, both physical and spiritual. But it is also a story that includes much conflict, as the change that has occurred in this man's life ripples out to his family, neighbors, and others in the Jewish community. First, we can imagine the incredible adjustment that the man himself would have experienced. His new sight would mean a loss of identity and income as someone who likely had only ever earned money from begging. As someone blind from birth, he would have to learn to navigate the physical world differently, now moving about as a seeing person. Such all-encompassing change is never easy. He would have to let go of his former life and begin to live in a whole new way. This disorientation and adjustment are a reality for many adult converts to Christianity, who must let go of some old and familiar ways and adopt new and strange ways.

New converts need to learn a new way of life, with different patterns of behavior and a new language. They learn to take their place in the body of Christ, the church. They learn to shape their lives around worship, study of the Scriptures, and prayer. As followers of Jesus, they learn about the importance of caring for the poor and marginalized. They learn about the rhythms, practices, and lexicon of whatever tradition of the church they begin to call home. They take on a new identity as one who has been forgiven and now serves the risen Lord. This process of change necessarily comes with some pain.

Second, we see that some pain emerges from the man's changed relationships with others, as his very identity was questioned following the healing. There were people who found it difficult to recognize this man apart from his blindness. His voice was the same. His body was largely the same. But now he could do much more than "sit and beg." Yet the text tells us he had to *repeatedly* tell them he was truly the man who had been healed. Some of them were still so suspicious that they took him to their religious leaders, the Pharisees, to confirm what had happened.

The conflict created by the man's change took a steep climb as division arose among the Pharisees. This in turn expanded the conflict outward as the parents of the man were brought into the synagogue for intense questioning. The joy of a miraculous healing appeared to be overshadowed by the need to confirm the man's identity and discuss doctrinal questions about what constituted correct observance of the Sabbath. There seems to have been agreement that making mud and applying it to someone's eyes constituted a breaking of Sabbath rules around work. The conflict, however, centered on how such a flagrant violation of Sabbath observance could have resulted in a healing. How could God have approved of this forbidden action by healing the man? How was Jesus of Nazareth, whom they were already suspicious of, involved? There was apparently much at risk, as the threat of being "put out of the synagogue" had already made the man's parents so fearful of the religious leaders that they deflected the questioning back to their son. This healing had resulted in conflict rippling out far beyond the man whom Jesus healed.

Such conflict can also occur with people who come to faith in Christ today. Conversion can bring pain to family and friends, whatever their faith background. How does the new Christian engage with their family during Jewish, Muslim, or Buddhist holidays and festivals? Such pain can also be experienced by converts from secular backgrounds, whose family or friends may be deeply suspicious of their newfound faith and the new practices it entails. While a fracturing of relationships is not always the outcome, there is often a period of adjustment on everyone's part, and that often involves pain.

The Promise of Conversion

There is also much promise in this story that informs our understanding of the promise of conversion. The formerly blind man had been given a change of status that was both mortal and eternal. He could now experience new independence and new possibilities due to his healed sight. He could walk alone if he so chose and explore wherever his curiosity might take him. He could, for the first time, see the beauty of palm trees blowing in the wind or sunlight glistening on a pool of water. He could see the enormous cut stones that formed the foundation of the temple and the beauty of the many archways framing the narrow streets of Jerusalem. He could look into the eyes of his parents.

The healing of this man's sight also brought another kind of seeing. He had seen Jesus, both physically and existentially, for the first time. He could experience a whole new community as part of the body of Christ, the community of Jesus's apprentices. He began to see clearly on both a physical and spiritual level. There's a beautiful symmetry in the text that begins with Jesus seeing this man and ends with the man seeing Jesus. The promise of conversion is new life itself, in and through Christ the Lord.

DISCUSSION QUESTIONS

1. If you became a Christian as an adult or came back to faith after a period away, share with the group the process by which that happened.
2. While some people come to faith quite suddenly, most do so over a period of time. What is the average length of time for the adult converts that you know?

3. How has your understanding of Jesus grown through the years?
4. Name two non-Christians in your life right now that you will commit to praying for and walking with so that they might come to see who Jesus is.

2

The Conversion of a Seeker Cut Off from God

Then an angel of the Lord said to Philip, "Get up and go toward the south to the road that goes down from Jerusalem to Gaza." (This is a wilderness road.) So he got up and went. Now there was an Ethiopian eunuch, a court official of the Candace, the queen of the Ethiopians, in charge of her entire treasury. He had come to Jerusalem to worship and was returning home; seated in his chariot, he was reading the prophet Isaiah. Then the Spirit said to Philip, "Go over to this chariot and join it." So Philip ran up to it and heard him reading the prophet Isaiah. He asked, "Do you understand what you are reading?" He replied, "How can I, unless someone guides me?" And he invited Philip to get in and sit beside him. Now the passage of the scripture that he was reading was this:

> "Like a sheep he was led to the slaughter,
> and like a lamb silent before its shearer,
> so he does not open his mouth.
> In his humiliation justice was denied him.
> Who can describe his generation?
> For his life is taken away from the earth."

The eunuch asked Philip, "About whom, may I ask you, does the prophet say this, about himself or about someone else?" Then Philip began to speak, and starting with this scripture he proclaimed to him the good news about Jesus. As they were going along the road, they came to some water, and the eunuch said, "Look, here is water! What is to prevent me from being baptized?" He commanded the chariot to stop, and both of them, Philip and the eunuch, went down into the water, and Philip baptized him. When they came up out of the water, the Spirit of the Lord snatched Philip away; the eunuch saw him no more and went on his way rejoicing.

—Acts 8:26–39

If there ever was a Bible passage to debunk the need for people to memorize a script or use a particular recipe to share the faith, the story of the first gentile conversion recorded in the book of Acts is surely it. This passage is full of extraordinary commands, a most unusual encounter, a weird but wonderful request, and then, just like that, it's over. No one could have predicted the flow or outcome of this story!

The Key Player

The Holy Spirit is the central player leading all the action in this story. First, the Lord sent an angel to direct Philip to go to a specific location at a specific time. Next, the Spirit pointed out to Philip whom he was to engage with. There, Philip encountered a man for whom the Spirit seemed to already have enlivened the written Word, quickening the man's curiosity to the point that he invited a complete stranger to join him in his chariot. The narrative ends with the Spirit snatching Philip away following the new convert's baptism. This conversion story makes one thing perfectly clear: God is the primary Evangelist. Philip, while obedient to the Spirit and definitely a participant, is simply trying his best to keep up with what God was doing. Surely this is the best sort of evangelism,

30

that which involves simply joining in the work God has already started and is directing.

Traits of an Evangelist

Having started with God's role, what can we now say about Philip? It can be very enriching to read through other Scripture passages that also mention a particular person. We learn some key information about Philip by looking through the book of Acts. In Acts 6:3 we learn that Philip was known as a person "of good standing, full of the Spirit and of wisdom." In 6:5 we learn that he was one of seven deacons chosen to serve the practical needs of poor widows within the believing community. In 8:5 we read that after the persecution and dispersion of Christians from Jerusalem, Philip traveled to Samaria to bring the people there the good news of Jesus the Messiah. We see from these references that Philip was both a person of good character and someone who demonstrated his love for Christ through words and deeds, even to people considered outside the fold, such as the Samaritans, who were avoided by Jews because they were considered heretics. This reaching out to outsiders continued throughout Philip's life. In 21:8–9 we learn that, about twenty years later, Philip was still being identified as "Philip the evangelist, one of the seven," who was now living in the coastal city of Caesarea and had passed the faith on to his four daughters (who, like their father, also "had the gift of prophecy").

Does Philip conform to what many Christians today consider to be an evangelist? There's no evidence he had an answer for every tough philosophical question. There's no indication that he was a brilliant communicator or charismatic extrovert. We aren't told whether he had success as a preacher to the Samaritans. What we do know is that he was someone who loved God, was attuned to and willing to follow the Spirit's lead, and wanted others to know the good news of Jesus. We are also told two other things about Philip: he was wise and he had a servant's heart.

Let's now consider another primary character in this story, the Ethiopian eunuch.

31

A Wealthy and Educated Man Cut Off from God

Of course, the most salient fact about this man is that he was a eunuch, since the passage mentions this five times in thirteen verses. What do we know about such people in the ancient world, and how might this factor into the conversion story? We learn from New Testament scholars that eunuchs were often deliberately castrated slaves, and they were among the most scorned members of society.[1] There were, however, at least two roles by which eunuchs could rise in status and power. They were often positioned as overseers of harems or as administrators working for queens or queen consorts. The latter was clearly the case with this man, for he was the overseer of the treasury for the Ethiopian queen, a role that would have conferred on him both wealth and power as a result of his close association with the royal court. As a eunuch he was not considered fully male in the ancient world. He would have posed no threat to the royal court, even though this was a society that rigidly protected access to high-status women and generally restricted social interaction between the sexes. The eunuch's possession of a scroll and his mode of transportation, in a chariot spacious enough for at least two passengers, is evidence of his wealth. Evidence of his education is seen in his ability to read a scroll in a language that was not his mother tongue.[2]

How did Judaism view and treat eunuchs? We know from Leviticus 21:17–20 that they were thought of as damaged goods and were not permitted to be priests. When the instructions for the ancient priesthood were given, the text records the Lord saying to Moses,

> Speak to Aaron and say: No one of your offspring throughout their generations who has a blemish may approach to offer the food of his God. Indeed, no one who has a blemish shall draw near, one who is blind or lame, or one who is mutilated or deformed, or one who has a broken foot or a broken hand, or a hunchback, or a dwarf, or a man with a defect in his eyes or an itching disease or scabs or crushed testicles. (Lev. 21:17–20)

1. Balz and Schneider, *Exegetical Dictionary of the New Testament*, 2:80–81.
2. Keener, *Acts*, 2:1585.

This prohibition against serving in the priesthood is expanded further in the book of Deuteronomy, which states, "No one whose testicles are crushed or whose penis is cut off shall come into the assembly of the LORD" (Deut. 23:1). While there is some debate among scholars as to what constituted "the assembly," there is agreement that eunuchs could be neither proselytes nor converts to Judaism.[3] This man's castration meant that ancient Judaism would have considered him to be cut off from God. Although the story tells us he had gone to Jerusalem to worship, was diligently reading from the Hebrew prophet Isaiah, and seems to have been a God-fearer and seeker, he would have *always* been considered a gentile, an outsider.

A Poignant Passage

We know little about the history of this Ethiopian.[4] He was likely forcibly castrated as a slave; it is also possible that he suffered an accident that resulted in castration. Least likely, he may have been born with what today would be called ambiguous genitalia. We simply don't know. We do know that he had no say in his condition and no power to change the stigmatization that was inextricably connected to it, both within Judaism and in the broader Greco-Roman culture. Because of his physical deformity, he was also cut off from God. He was relegated to being part of a ridiculed and despised group. He would never have children to carry his name into the next generation. And he simply had no say in any of this.

Let's now consider the passage the Ethiopian eunuch was reading.

> Like a sheep he was led to the slaughter,
> and like a lamb silent before its shearer,
> so he does not open his mouth.

3. Keener, *Acts*, 2:1566.
4. The Greek word for "Ethiopian" referred more generally to African lands south of Egypt but especially to Nubia. Keener, *Acts*, 2:1550.

> In his humiliation justice was denied him.
>> Who can describe his generation?
>>> For his life is taken away from the earth. (Isa. 53:7–8,
>>>> quoted in Acts 8:32–33)

Is it any wonder this passage caught his attention and resonated so deeply? While we can't know what this man was thinking, we can guess why the Ethiopian asked Philip, "About whom, may I ask you, does the prophet say this, about himself or about someone else?" (8:34). How could Isaiah, a prophet of God, understand so deeply what this eunuch himself felt? Or did the prophet know another who was so despised and rejected, so wrongly judged and shamed? About whom was the prophet speaking?

Good News for the Suffering

Philip's response is summed up in one sentence in this story: "Then Philip began to speak, and starting with this scripture he proclaimed to him the good news about Jesus" (8:35). Christians looking for a script for sharing the gospel will be disappointed, for Philip took quite a different approach: listening first, asking if help was needed, awaiting an invitation, and responding to a question only with what he knew about Jesus, the person who Christians throughout the ages have identified as fulfilling Isaiah 53. One who suffered at the hands of others. One who suffered humiliation. One for whom justice was denied. One whose life was taken from him.

And yet that was not the end of the story for the one written about by the prophet, as Philip must have conveyed. The resurrection of Jesus turned his humiliation and death upside down. What looked like a horrible defeat was revealed to be an ultimate victory. The victory of God. The good news. God, in Christ, had atoned for the sin of all the ages, and he was now reconciling the whole world to himself. I often wonder if Philip showed the Ethiopian eunuch a passage in Isaiah located just three chapters after the passage he was reading. If he did, it would surely be part of the good news that Philip spoke of that day. Isaiah's long-promised Suffering Servant had come, and as a result everything had changed.

> Do not let the foreigner joined to the LORD say,
>> "The LORD will surely separate me from his people,"
> and do not let the eunuch say,
>> "I am just a dry tree."
> For thus says the LORD:
> To the eunuchs who keep my Sabbaths,
>> who choose the things that please me
>> and hold fast my covenant,
> I will give, in my house and within my walls,
>> a monument and a name
>> better than sons and daughters;
> I will give them an everlasting name
>> that shall not be cut off. (Isa. 56:3–8)

The story of the Ethiopian eunuch in Acts takes place among a series of stories about the sharing of the gospel with more and more outsiders. Philip seems to have been particularly called to this work. First we read about him preaching to the Samaritans. Next we learn about him discipling and baptizing Simon, who was formerly a sorcerer. This conversion is followed by him being sent to reach the Ethiopian eunuch, after which he was whisked away to the city of Azotus and then to villages and towns up the Mediterranean coast, until he finally reached Caesarea, where he settled. The church in Jerusalem may have been persecuted and scattered, but it was now reaching farther and farther out across the ancient world.

Loving God as the Starting Point

When churches think about how to encourage their members to share the faith, they often start looking for a new program or the latest resources in evangelism. Yet this story, and most other conversion stories in the Bible, suggests that evangelism begins with something else entirely: a deep love for God that results in a commitment to spending time with God. Our efforts to cultivate missional churches must begin with teaching our people that the Christian disciplines of silence, solitude, meditation, and prayer are the birthing ground for sharing the gospel with others. Philip's amazing interaction with the Ethiopian eunuch began with hearing something, an instruction from an angel of the Lord.

In the West, these spiritual disciplines have often been viewed merely as the way we ourselves are fed in the faith, and so they have become disconnected from the church's calling to share the gospel. But if we don't see these disciplines as attending to God, how can we be attentive to God's prodding, direction, and guidance in sharing the faith? The Ethiopian eunuch came to know about God's amazing love for him demonstrated in the life of Jesus, the Suffering Servant, because Philip *heard* God's direction. As we see in so many biblical conversion stories, and as we see in research on churches that are effectively reaching new people today, learning to listen for God's direction is key.[5] God most desires us to be a people of prayer. The Great Evangelist wants to teach and guide us, if we only make listening and speaking with him a priority, not just for our own sake but for the sake of the world God loves. As we seek to be a people who reach out with the gospel, our first question should be, Is this goal grounded in a deep love for God as evidenced in a commitment to prayer?

Loving People outside the Church

This brings us to the second question the church needs to ask itself: Do we really love those outside the church? Most churches would affirm this as a worthy goal and something they endeavor to do. And yet if we examine our church budgets, or the amount of time spent interacting with or serving those in our neighborhood, or the number of friendships we have with non-Christian or dechurched people, it's tough to see the evidence for how we

5. In her research into mainline churches that are reaching new people with the gospel, Martha Grace Reece discovered the key role of a deep commitment to prayer. See Reece, *Unbinding the Gospel*, 41–56.

truly love those outside the church. Do we love them by seeing them as people who may have a private love for God that they've never talked about with anyone? Do we love them by seeing them as people with many of the same sorrows we experience in life but without the hope of the gospel? Do we love them by thinking of outsiders as people who have a hunger for God that they cannot yet name?

The Ethiopian eunuch was a man largely cut off from God, according to the rules of first-century Judaism. Similarly, there are many people today who feel cut off from God. Some are all too aware of their own failings and cannot imagine themselves being accepted in the community of faith. Some, having never learned that God is *both* merciful and just, assume they could never be good enough for God. Some think that those who go to church are either self-righteous hypocrites or people who are truly more holy than they are, and so they can't see themselves ever belonging to a church. Some, having learned plenty about the historical failings of the church, simply doubt the existence of a community that truly embodies the love, joy, peace, patience, kindness, goodness, faithfulness, gentleness, and self-control of God.

Philip obeyed the Spirit's prodding to go from where he was because he heard that God had someone for him to minister to. God had a deep love for the Ethiopian eunuch, a wealthy yet despised outsider with spiritual questions and longings. Churches that want to follow God's lead in sharing the gospel need first to follow God's heart by loving those outside the church.

A Process That Depends on God and Respects People

Strangely, many in the church today imagine that effective evangelism is all about telling. But this story suggests that before the telling comes listening, obeying, and listening again. Philip listened and obeyed God by going to the outsider. He listened again to what the Ethiopian was reading. This would be trickier in our culture today since most people now read silently. But in the ancient world reading was most often done aloud. This allowed Philip to discern a bridge into this man's life, a bridge that came in the form of a question. Did the Ethiopian understand what he was reading?

Philip's listening, followed by a well-placed and thoughtful question, was the basis for the Ethiopian inviting Philip to join him in his chariot for a conversation (a considerable honor in the ancient world). Similarly, we too can be listening to the sorts of things we hear outsiders focusing on and questioning, and we can join them in their curiosity and exploration.

The Compelling Written Word

Our willingness to listen is an indication of something else: a recognition that God is already present and at work in someone's life. The Ethiopian had already been led to read the words of the prophet Isaiah, and they were words that made him curious. We don't know where this man got a precious scroll of the book of Isaiah. As a manuscript of the ancient world, it would have been handwritten, letter by letter, with meticulous precision. This made such manuscripts both rare and costly. Perhaps he purchased it during his visit to Jerusalem. Ultimately, we don't know *where or when he got it*, but we do know *why he was reading it*: the Holy Spirit was enlivening the written Word and drawing the man to himself. Imagine if Christians viewed everyone outside the church, whether rich or poor, through this lens, as people in whom God was already at work in some way. What if we invited our non-Christian friends to read and discuss passages from Scripture, believing that God can mysteriously bring his written Word to life for anyone?

Focusing on Christ

Although the Ethiopian was reading from the book of Isaiah, Philip chose to focus on Christ. Surely, he could have answered the eunuch's question by describing the prophet's life and ministry. Or he could have focused on the story of Israel. Alternatively, he could have taken the moralistic approach and directed the man to the passage of promise for eunuchs in Isaiah 56:4, calling him to be one of those eunuchs who keep the Lord's sabbath, choose the things that please God, and hold fast to God's covenant.

Instead Philip chose a much different approach. He directed the man's attention to Jesus Christ as the central figure in the grand narrative of God's work of reconciling the world to himself. He told him why this person, Jesus, was good news for both the eunuch and the whole world. Philip used the Scripture that the man asked about, a passage so deeply linked to our Lord's suffering and death, to point him to Jesus. Throughout the conversation, Philip knew how to let the main thing be the main thing.

At the heart of the Christian faith is a person, not a list of propositions or practices. Such things can help us in our walk as Christians, but we must not confuse them with the person of Christ. Thousands of years after his death, Jesus is still a compelling figure. He has been depicted in countless stained-glass windows, paintings, and carvings. Images of him have graced the covers of countless books and magazines. Hundreds, perhaps thousands, of films have been made based on his life and teachings. Today, people are much more interested in the person at the heart of the Christian faith than they are in the institution that developed around him. When we engage people in conversation about their spiritual questions and longings, we should remember Philip and the way he pointed directly to the person and work of Jesus as the good news that he had to share.

Calling for a Response

We are given few details about the conversation between these two men. What exactly did Philip say about Jesus? We don't know. But we can gather that, at some point, he must have mentioned the Christian sacrament of baptism, because this is what the Ethiopian suggested should be his response to the good news that Philip conveyed. The description of this baptism is beautiful. The chariot of this official of the Ethiopian court stops near a pool of water. Philip and the new convert go down into the water, and Philip performs what will become the central rite of initiation into the Christian faith across the eons.

A sacrament has been defined as "an outward and visible sign of inward and spiritual grace."[6] Sacraments are much more than a physical act we participate in, more than just our response to something. Yet they do require us to do certain physical things, such as being immersed in or sprinkled with water, or consuming bread and wine. Whatever response is required, that response is a response to the grace of God. When we witness to the good news of Jesus, we should remember that, at some point, we are hoping that person will *respond* to God's gift of grace. Historically, that response has been more than simply praying a certain prayer or thinking a certain thought. Historically, that response to God's grace has been participation in the sacrament of baptism.

Understanding Brokenness

Finally, this story reminds us to have a right understanding of the brokenness of this world and of God's power to reach into and redeem that brokenness. Who are the people all around us in our towns, cities, places of work, and families who feel cut off from God and beyond the reach of faith? What new life can take root in them as they discover they are loved and valued by the creator of reality itself? There is a lostness that can only be remedied by being found in Christ. Until the church takes that lostness seriously, it is unlikely to do the work of evangelism. However, if we become a praying church, directed by God and a love for the lost, we will again experience the joy that both Philip and the Ethiopian knew that day on the road to Gaza.

6. Attributed to St. Augustine, this definition can be found in Anglican Church of Canada, *Book of Common Prayer*, 550.

DISCUSSION QUESTIONS

1. Does your church pray each week for people who feel cut off from God? If not, why do you think that is?
2. What would you most want your non-Christian friends to know about Jesus?
3. Have you ever asked a non-Christian friend to read and discuss together some Scripture passages from the first biographies of Jesus? (If not, have a look at the appendix, which describes some experiments churches can try as they learn to better connect with non-Christians and introduce them to the Christian faith.)

3

The Conversion of Friends, Family, and Students

The next day John again was standing with two of his disciples, and as he watched Jesus walk by he exclaimed, "Look, here is the Lamb of God!" The two disciples heard him say this, and they followed Jesus. When Jesus turned and saw them following, he said to them, "What are you looking for?" They said to him, "Rabbi" (which translated means Teacher), "where are you staying?" He said to them, "Come and see." They came and saw where he was staying, and they remained with him that day. It was about four o'clock in the afternoon. One of the two who heard John speak and followed him was Andrew, Simon Peter's brother. He first found his brother Simon and said to him, "We have found the Messiah" (which is translated Anointed). He brought Simon to Jesus, who looked at him and said, "You are Simon son of John. You are to be called Cephas" (which is translated Peter).

The next day Jesus decided to go to Galilee. He found Philip and said to him, "Follow me." Now Philip was from Bethsaida, the city of Andrew and Peter. Philip found Nathanael and said to him, "We have found him about whom Moses in the Law and also the Prophets wrote, Jesus son of Joseph from Nazareth." Nathanael said to him, "Can anything good come out of Nazareth?" Philip said to him, "Come and see." When Jesus saw Nathanael coming toward him, he said of him, "Here is truly an Israelite in whom there is no deceit!" Nathanael asked him, "Where did you get to know me?" Jesus answered, "I saw you under the fig tree before Philip called you." Nathanael replied, "Rabbi, you are the Son of God! You are the King of Israel!" Jesus answered, "Do you believe because I told you that I saw you under the fig tree? You will see greater things than these." And he said to him, "Very truly, I tell you, you will see heaven opened and the angels of God ascending and descending upon the Son of Man."

—John 1:35–51

I t's clear from the conversion stories of Scripture that there are many paths to faith in Jesus, but underlying these different journeys are also some common characteristics. One commonality is that deep relationships often pave the way for the transmission of the gospel. In the above passage we see a teacher telling students, brother telling brother, and friend telling friend. A great question for Christians to ask themselves is, Who among my colleagues, neighbors, family, and friends could I invite to "come and see" Jesus?

The Important Soil of Relationships

The story begins with John the Baptist pointing his own disciples to Jesus, whom he describes as the Lamb of God. Viewed as a compelling preacher and prophet in his own right, John nonetheless continued to point not to himself but to Jesus, stating simply, "He must increase, but I must decrease" (John 3:30). John's public ministry, preceding that of Jesus's ministry, would indeed decline. Yet it was out of the rich relationship between John and his disciples that a word of witness was given and received, stimulating curiosity about Jesus. John's influence over his disciples cascaded into others coming to know Jesus, as Andrew invited his brother Simon to also come and see. The text further tells us that these two brothers came from Bethsaida, a village located on the shores of the Sea of Galilee.

Bethsaida was also the home of another man whom Andrew and Simon Peter would almost certainly have known well, Philip. When Philip encountered Jesus, his first response was to tell his friend Nathanael, who, while initially skeptical, was completely won over by Jesus's insight and foreknowledge of both Nathanael's character and even his prior whereabouts. But what can we say about Jesus's own use of relationship building to disciple people?

Come, See, Follow

The initial interaction between John's disciples and Jesus seems almost comical to our modern ears. They couldn't think of a better question to ask the man they had been told was the Lamb of God than "Where are you staying?" Seriously? Were they caught off guard when Jesus saw them following him and asked, "What are you looking for?" (1:38)? Was their response the kind of awkward question that can pop out of your mouth that you immediately regret? Was the disciple who asked it jabbed in the ribs by his traveling companion? We'll never know. But perhaps there is more to this question than meets the eye.

The relationship between rabbi and disciple in first-century Judaism was cultivated by being together. They had been with John, who had pointed them to Jesus. Now they wanted to learn about and learn from this Jesus of Nazareth, who John had told them was the Lamb of God. Perhaps it was not an awkward question after all. Perhaps in that culture it was a perfectly normal question to ask someone whom you wanted to learn from. Jesus seems to treat it as such. First, Jesus turned and saw them. Then, he asked them what they were looking for. When they replied with their own question about where he was staying, he replied simply, "Come and see" (1:39). In short, he invited them to accompany him. This progression of first being seen by Jesus and then being invited to come, see, and follow is the journey that so many people take in coming to know Jesus.

45

What did they come to know about this person Jesus, son of Joseph from Nazareth? The descriptors used for Jesus in this short conversion story are rich and varied. In the space of just seventeen verses, Jesus is referred to as Lamb of God, Rabbi, Messiah, Son of God, King of Israel, and Son of Man. Having only just met Jesus, these Jewish men already identified him as the one "about whom Moses in the Law and also the Prophets wrote" (1:44). But they really began to know him as they journeyed, ate, and lived with him; they also learned from him and even received a new name from him. It's more of an apprenticeship model of learning than a contemporary classroom model of learning. The apprenticeship model assumes that authentic and deep relationship is the normative ground in which the gospel is planted.

What could this model look like in our world today, and what can we learn about evangelism from this conversion story?

Preceding Spiritual Lives

Many people already have spiritual questions and longings and are already engaging in religious practices such as prayer prior to becoming Christians. Andrew was already a disciple of John the Baptist, as were many other people who eventually became Christians. In Acts 19:1–7 we read about the apostle Paul encountering a small group of "disciples" in Corinth. As Paul got to know these people, he realized that they were not yet followers of Jesus.

> He said to them, "Did you receive the Holy Spirit when you became believers?" They replied, "No, we have not even heard that there is a Holy Spirit." Then he said, "Into what, then, were you baptized?" They answered, "Into John's baptism." Paul said, "John baptized with the baptism of repentance, telling the people to believe in the one who was to come after him, that is, in Jesus." On hearing this, they were baptized in the name of the Lord Jesus. When Paul had laid his hands on them, the Holy Spirit came upon them, and they spoke in tongues and prophesied, altogether there were about twelve of them. (Acts 19:2–7)

As in the case of Andrew, the preceding spiritual life of the people in Corinth set the stage for their acceptance of the good news of Jesus Christ. This phenomenon has been repeated throughout the history of Christianity.

George Hunter's book *The Celtic Way of Evangelism* explores the ways in which practices of first-millennium Celtic missionaries have relevance for transmission of the Christian faith today. Pointing to the scholarly work of Brendan Lehane's *The Quest of Three Abbots*, Hunter argues that religious beliefs, practices, and artifacts already present in the pre-Christian Celtic culture prepared the ground for the evangelization of the Celts. This included such things as standing-stone circles, a reverence for spiritual narratives and poems, triads, an acceptance of paradox, links between spirituality and creation, and an emphasis on community. These cultural traits lent themselves well to the introduction of Christian beliefs, practices, and religious items.

Standing stones prefigured standing-stone crosses. The gospel narratives fit well with an already-existing love of stories. And Christian teachings, such as the doctrine of the Trinity, the immanence and transcendence of God, the incarnation, and the church as the body of Christ, also found bridges in Celtic belief in a physically grounded and communal spirituality that allowed room for paradox.[1]

Christians would do well to attend to the broader beliefs and interests today that may serve as a bridge by which people will hear and respond to the Christian message. For example, many people who consider themselves spiritual but not religious believe in some form of reincarnation. While reincarnation is certainly not a Christian belief, the underlying longing for life beyond death provides a bridge to discuss Christian teachings about the resurrection and Jesus's conquering of the grave. Can we attend more closely to where the Holy Spirit has gone ahead of us, preparing the soil for planting gospel seeds? The Celtic Christian missionaries used many cultural bridges for the gospel. Could

---

1. Hunter, *Celtic Way of Evangelism*, 8.

the rising interest, particularly among Millennials and Gen Z, in the environment, local food production, mental health, and social justice issues be meaningfully engaged as we explore with them the teachings of Scripture, and particularly those of Jesus, with the hope that they will come into a living relationship with him?

Many Diverse Journeys

A second truth about evangelism we see in this passage from John's Gospel is that God uses many methods to reconcile people with himself. Some people heard about Jesus through people they already knew. For example, John describes Jesus to his two disciples, and Philip invites Nathanael to "come and see." But other people experienced the call to "come and see" directly from Jesus. In our own time this can happen through people experiencing dreams and visions of Jesus. One man I know came to follow Jesus because of seeing him while in a coma following a serious car accident.

As a pastor I have heard many stories of people who felt compelled to explore Christianity because of a film they saw or a book they read. One couple began their journey to faith as a result of watching the televised wedding of the Prince and Princess of Wales. I know a woman who came back to faith, after many years away, because she heard Christmas carols being sung as she stood on the sidewalk outside a church on a snowy Christmas Eve. Even more strangely, someone I know started on their journey to Jesus because they found themselves repeatedly waking up at 3:33 a.m. Another person began their journey as a result of a backlit stained-glass window. And someone else started exploring because a piece of trash blew onto their apartment balcony. These are all stories I have heard as just one pastor among tens of thousands of pastors across North America. Such stories remind me that God is continually active in this world, drawing people to himself and reconciling the world to himself one human heart at a time.

Discipleship Starts with a Community

A third lesson about evangelism that can be drawn from this story is that God uses communities of faith in the process of evangelization and discipleship. Jesus called his first disciples to come and live together as a community, even though they were people who under normal circumstances were unlikely to have had anything to do with one another. Matthew, a tax collector for the occupying Romans, became part of a community of people who were being brutally oppressed by those same Romans. The earliest church was led by Galilean fishermen like Peter and pedigreed Jewish scholars like Paul. They didn't always agree on things, as various New Testament passages make clear,[2] but they were a community, the church, and they found their common purpose in the transmission of the good news of the kingdom of God. The *missio Dei*, the mission of God, was at their community's heart.

In his exploration of how Celtic missionaries spread the gospel so effectively, Hunter points to the centrality of mission among the communities founded by those Celtic missionaries. He contrasts what he calls the Roman Model of evangelism (presentation, decision, assimilation) with a much different three-part Celtic Model:

> (1) Establish community with people or bring them into the fellowship of your community of faith; (2) within fellowship, engage in conversation, ministry, prayer, and worship; and (3) in time, as they discover that they now believe, invite them to commit.[3]

In this model, belonging precedes believing. Perhaps this first-millennium approach can again help new people come to faith in the third millennium. In a world characterized by high rates of global migration and personal transience, perhaps by refocusing on inviting people into Christian communities, they will come to believe in Christ and learn the new countercultural behaviors of the Christian life.

2. See Acts 6, 15, and Phil. 2.
3. Hunter, *Celtic Way of Evangelism*, 43.

The Verbs of Discipleship

A final lesson in this biblical conversion story focuses on the purpose of formation in the Christian life. By paying attention to the verbs used in this passage, we see that personal formation is the goal. But this goal is undertaken for the sake of the world. Someone comes, sees, finds, and follows, and then passes that witness on to others so that they too can "come and see."

Throughout the whole biblical narrative, the passing on of a blessing is at the core of the community of God's people. God blesses Abraham so that he might become a blessing to all nations. Note the end goal: "I will make of you a great nation, and I will bless you and make your name great, so that you will be a blessing" (Gen. 12:2). Likewise, Jesus calls and sends out seventy-two of his first followers so that others may hear and know that the kingdom of God has come near and may hear a word of peace proclaimed and receive healing (Luke 10:1–9). As Hunter describes the end goal of the Celtic missionaries, evangelism and discipleship are ultimately about the reconciliation of the whole world by the transformation of every human heart.

> Our formation is for the sake of ministry and mission; most of our needs are met as we lose ourselves for the sake of Christ and his reign in human experience and human affairs. We are incrementally and over time, formed in the likeness of Christ in order to be liberated from our self-interest and narcissism and, more important, to be given the credibility, the compassion, and the power from which ministry and mission make a difference.[4]

If we claim to be followers of Christ, we need to see discipleship more like Jesus did: less about packaged programs, resources, and methods, and more about relationships marked by seeing, inviting, and being together as communities of faith so that people may come to know Jesus as the Teacher, the Messiah, the Son of God, the Son of Man, the King of Israel, and Lord of their lives, just as John, Andrew, Peter, Philip, and Nathanael did.

4. Hunter, *Celtic Way of Evangelism*, 99.

DISCUSSION QUESTIONS

1. Who first taught you about Jesus?
2. Describe the first church that you belonged to.
3. How did that community of faith disciple you? Did it begin with teaching or with relationship?
4. Who among your family, friends, and colleagues would you like to help know Jesus better?

4

The Conversion of a God-Fearing Outsider

In Caesarea there was a man named Cornelius, a centurion of the Italian Cohort, as it was called. He was a devout man who feared God with all his household; he gave alms generously to the people and prayed constantly to God. One afternoon at about three o'clock he had a vision in which he clearly saw an angel of God coming in and saying to him, "Cornelius." He stared at him in terror and said, "What is it, Lord?" He answered, "Your prayers and your alms have ascended as a memorial before God. Now send men to Joppa for a certain Simon who is called Peter; he is lodging with Simon, a tanner, whose house is by the seaside." When the angel who spoke to him had left, he called two of his slaves and a devout soldier from the ranks of those who served him, and after telling them everything he sent them to Joppa.

About noon the next day, as they were on their journey and approaching the city, Peter went up on the roof to pray. He became hungry and wanted something to eat, and while it was being prepared he fell into a trance. He saw the heaven opened and something like a large sheet coming down, being lowered to the ground by its four corners. In it were all kinds of four-footed creatures and reptiles and birds of the air. Then he heard a voice saying,

"Get up, Peter; kill and eat." But Peter said, "By no means, Lord, for I have never eaten anything that is profane or unclean." The voice said to him again, a second time, "What God has made clean, you must not call profane." This happened three times, and the thing was suddenly taken up to heaven.

Now while Peter was greatly puzzled about what to make of the vision that he had seen, suddenly the men sent by Cornelius appeared. They were asking for Simon's house and were standing by the gate. They called out to ask whether Simon, who was called Peter, was staying there. While Peter was still thinking about the vision, the Spirit said to him, "Look, three men are searching for you. Now get up, go down, and go with them without hesitation, for I have sent them." So Peter went down to the men and said, "I am the one you are looking for; what is the reason for your coming?" They answered, "Cornelius, a centurion, a righteous and God-fearing man who is well spoken of by the whole Jewish people, was directed by a holy angel to send for you to come to his house and to hear what you have to say." So Peter invited them in and gave them lodging.

The next day he got up and went with them, and some of the brothers and sisters from Joppa accompanied him. The following day they came to Caesarea. Cornelius was expecting them and had called together his relatives and close friends. On Peter's arrival, Cornelius met him and, falling at his feet, worshiped him. But Peter made him get up, saying, "Stand up; I am only a mortal." And as he talked with him, he went in and found that many had assembled, and he said to them, "You yourselves know that it is improper for a Jew to associate with or to visit an outsider, but God has shown me that I should not call anyone profane or unclean. So when I was sent for, I came without objection. Now may I ask why you sent for me?"

Cornelius replied, "Four days ago at this very hour, at three o'clock, I was praying in my house when suddenly a man in dazzling clothes stood before me. He said, 'Cornelius, your prayer has been heard, and your alms have been remembered before God. Send therefore to Joppa and ask for Simon, who is called Peter; he is staying in the home of Simon, a tanner, by the sea.' Therefore I sent for you immediately, and you have been kind enough to come. So now all of us are here in the presence of God to listen to all that the Lord has commanded you to say."

Then Peter began to speak to them: "I truly understand that God shows no partiality, but in every people anyone who fears him and practices righteousness is acceptable to him. You know the message he sent to the people of Israel, preaching peace by Jesus Christ—he is Lord of all. That message spread throughout Judea, beginning in Galilee after the baptism that John announced: how God anointed Jesus of Nazareth with the Holy Spirit and with power; how he went about doing good and healing all who were oppressed by the devil, for God was with him. We are witnesses to all that he did both in Judea and in Jerusalem. They put him to death by hanging him on a tree, but God raised him on the third day and allowed him to appear, not to all the people but to us who were chosen by God as witnesses and who ate and drank with him after he rose from the dead. He commanded us to preach to the people and to testify that he is the one ordained by God as judge of the living and the dead. All the prophets testify about him that everyone who believes in him receives forgiveness of sins through his name."

While Peter was still speaking, the Holy Spirit fell upon all who heard the word. The circumcised believers who had come with Peter were astounded that the gift of the Holy Spirit had been poured out even on the gentiles, for they heard them speaking in tongues and extolling God. Then Peter said, "Can anyone withhold the water for baptizing these people who have received the Holy Spirit just as we have?" So he ordered them to be baptized in the name of Jesus Christ. Then they invited him to stay for several days.

—Acts 10:1–48

The story of Cornelius's conversion turns upside down so many assumptions about how evangelism works. One assumption is that we need to go out and share the gospel with those who don't know Jesus. Yet in this story we see Peter, someone who knows Jesus well, being diligently sought out by Cornelius, someone who doesn't know Jesus at all. Another assumption is that we share the gospel so that people can come to know God, receive his forgiveness, learn his ways, and live as his holy people. Holiness, demonstrated through the fruit of the Spirit

(Gal. 5:22–23), is the goal of discipleship, isn't it? Except here we see Cornelius, the one who has yet to hear the gospel, described as a devout God-fearer and someone who regularly prays and cares for the poor. What is going on?

The Preexisting Spiritual Lives of People outside the Faith

This conversion story yet again brings to light another important truth: people often have a spiritual life that may prepare them to hear and accept the gospel. We aren't told how Cornelius became a God-fearer. We aren't told when he first prayed. We aren't told why he gave generously to those in need. But we *are* told that Cornelius's actions pleased God immensely. In fact, Cornelius's prayers and good deeds had "ascended as a memorial before God" (10:4). In other words, they were a pleasing offering in God's eyes, given by someone who had yet to hear about Christ.

Sadly, would-be evangelists often have faulty assumptions concerning the spiritual lives of non-Christians that prevent them from effectively sharing the gospel. How much better it would be if Christians took the time to respectfully discover what people believe and find bridges for telling others about Jesus. I once had a student who submitted a paper focused on Christian apologetic arguments disproving the foundational beliefs of Islam. While these were well-formed and potentially convincing arguments, when I asked the student what she saw within Islam that might be a bridge for sharing the good news of Jesus, the student drew a complete blank. She had spent so much time disproving what she saw as erroneous beliefs in Islam that she failed to discover even a single possible bridge within Muslims' preexisting spiritual frameworks for sharing the gospel. Such bridges include a recognition of the goodness of God's creation, the importance of prayer, a reverence for and interest in Jesus, and the call to live an upright and moral life, which includes care for the poor.

As Christians we must not deny the real differences between Christianity and other belief systems, and we want people everywhere to come to know the saving grace that is available through Christ alone. But if we trust that God is already at work in people's lives and we demonstrate this trust in conversation, we might well be granted a hearing rather than be quickly dismissed. Perhaps God is already speaking to that person, calling them, revealing himself to them in new and even puzzling ways, as he did for Cornelius. What if we focused first not on their lack of knowledge of Christ but on the spiritual experiences, convictions, longings, and prayers that might prove to be a bridge for introducing them to him?

Between 2017 and 2022 a series of Angus Reid nationwide opinion polls conducted across Canada revealed some remarkable data. Though only 18 percent of Canadians have any substantive connection to a faith community, 21 percent of the total population were categorized as "privately faithful," based on their beliefs, behaviors, and attitudes concerning faith. Despite having little to no connection to a faith community, a solid majority of this group were found to pray regularly, believe that God is active in the world, wish they had a closer relationship with God, and want their children to be taught about God by a faith community. This group represents over 7.5 million Canadians who have a significant preexisting spiritual life. Furthermore, this research indicated that an additional 42 percent of Canadians fit into a group they labeled "spiritually uncertain." This group was generally quite unsure about the existence of God and rarely prayed, but they did express spiritual questions and longings. This group represents almost 16 million people. Only 18 percent of the Canadian population were revealed to be ardent nonbelievers, based on these polls.[1]

One way to reach people who are privately faithful or spiritually uncertain is to get to know them, learn about what they currently believe, and consider how those ideas and practices might form

1. Ray Pennings and Jenisa Los, "The Shifting Landscape of Faith in Canada," Cardus, 2022, p. 13, https://www.cardus.ca/research/spirited-citizenship/reports/the-shifting-landscape-of-faith-in-canada.

a bridge for the gospel. To do this, the church will need to reach out beyond its own walls.

Are such people interested in meditation? Given the rich history of Christian meditation extending back across two millennia, why not offer a class on Christian meditation at a local community center? If they want their kids to learn the real story of Christmas or the basics of the Christian faith, why not offer a craft series for parents and kids in the neighborhood to focus on this, or host a live nativity play in a local park? Do people sense God's presence when out in nature? Why not offer a trail walk that exposes them to the many passages of Scripture that talk about God as the creator of all that is seen and unseen? Above all, let's assume that the non-Christians we meet are not simply physical, emotional, and intellectual beings but also spiritual beings whom God is already calling to himself.

God's Prevenient Grace in the Lives of Seekers

A second and related truth in the story of Cornelius's conversion is that God was already at work paving the way for Cornelius to receive the good news of Jesus. The ancient church doctrine of prevenient grace refers to the grace of God that "goes before" salvation: God's gracious presence and work in the lives of people who don't yet fully recognize him. While this doctrine was particularly highlighted in the teaching and preaching of John Wesley, it can be traced much further back in time, being expounded on in the canons of the Council of Orange in AD 529, and some version of this doctrine is held across all Christian denominations.

Indeed, in the story of Cornelius's conversion, God's prevenient grace shows up in many ways as he sends angelic messengers, gives dreams and visions, stirs up curiosity, orchestrates meetings, and gifts people with startling experiences of his Holy Spirit. Isn't this just like God? No matter the age we ourselves became followers of Jesus, we can always point to the way God was at work in our lives well ahead of any decision we made.

Yet despite our recognition of this grace going before us in our own lives, we often behave as if the success or failure of sharing the gospel rests entirely on us having the right words, arguments, tactics, or skills. The text says Peter simply went up on the roof to pray. Maybe one of the most important ways we can prepare to more effectively share the faith is to be like Peter and set aside time to pray.

Before starting any evangelistic endeavor, let's pray first that God will help us attend to God so that we rightly discern the path he wants us to take. "Lord, give me clear direction for where you are calling me to go." Let's pray that God will help us attend to the people he places in our path and who are hungry to hear the good news of Jesus. "Lord, may I hear those you have sent and who are knocking at the door." Let's pray that he will give us willing hearts to venture into places and lives that may be very different from our own, for the sake of the gospel. "Lord, make me ready to go where I haven't gone before." Let's pray that he will give us a clear word of witness that points people to Jesus. "Lord, may Jesus always be at the forefront of my witness." Let's pray that his Holy Spirit will enable and empower new life. "Lord, may your presence and power be known to those we witness to." Let's heed Peter's example, understanding that the ongoing witness of the church needs to be grounded in attending to and following God's lead, which can only happen by making prayer the highest priority as the foundation of all evangelism.

God Is the Primary Evangelist

As the previous conversion stories have also highlighted, the story of Cornelius's conversion points to God himself as the primary Evangelist. God wants to be known, and he is tirelessly creative in drawing us to him. Isn't it startling that he invites us to join in his mission? This story shows how many people God is willing to include in his work. For this is a story not simply about Peter's witness to Cornelius. This is a story of God making himself known to many, including the Caesarean centurion (10:1), two of his servants and one of his soldiers (v. 7), as well as the large gathering of people who were present at Cornelius's house to greet Peter on the day of his arrival (v. 27).

We can't be sure how many believed and were baptized because of Peter's message about Jesus and the astonishing manifestation of the Holy Spirit, but Peter's order that they be baptized certainly suggests it was most of those in attendance. Apparently, God was at work in many people's lives that day, and little details in the text point to the centrality of the triune God's activity in the story. For instance, why are there so many threes mentioned? Cornelius's vision of the angel occurred at three in the afternoon. He sent three men to search for Peter. Peter's vision of the sheet of nonkosher foods occurred three times. And Cornelius noted that it was three days from the time of his angelic vision to Peter sharing the gospel with him and his household. Was the trinitarian God leaving his fingerprint as the primary mover over every part of this story? Surely God's own activity was the only thing that could explain the extraordinary chain of events that took place.

As Christians, our understanding of how to share the faith changes when we see that God is the primary Evangelist and we are simply invited to join in the work he is already doing in people's lives. That perspective changes everything. What we often treat as a risky and onerous duty turns into an adventure in attending to, and joining, God's activity.

Dreams and Visions as Instruments of God

A fourth key element in this conversion story is the extraordinary mystical phenomena. An angel gave travel directions, a vision changed a leader's ideas of who was acceptable to God, and a houseful of people suddenly praised God in previously unknown languages. Particularly in the West, where the church has been deeply affected by Enlightenment assumptions about reality, knowledge, and rationality, perhaps Christians have come to think of evangelism as scripted, argument-based, and managed. Perhaps we are even a little threatened by an uncontrollable God who is not above using extraordinary means to reach people.

Regardless of our comfort level, God continues to use dreams and visions to reach new people with news about what he has done for the world through Jesus Christ. For several decades Christian missionaries across the Middle East have been reporting that Muslims have been having dreams and visions of Jesus, afterward seeking out Christians who can help explain who he is.[2] Similarly, in a survey of 750 people who had converted from Islam to Christianity between 1991 and 2007, researchers found that 27 percent of these new converts reported having dreams and visions prior to becoming Christians, and a full 40 percent had these at the time of conversion.[3] It would seem that the kind of dreams and visions involved in Cornelius's conversion are not so strange after all; they are tools God still uses today.

Attentive Obedience and Evangelism

A fifth key lesson is that submission and obedience are required of both evangelist and seeker. Cornelius needed to heed and obey the direction given to him by the angelic visitor in his vision. Peter needed to obey the command in his threefold vision of the descending and ascending sheet and the subsequent instructions. Both men had to obey God's direction, and for both this meant venturing into uncharted territory. Cornelius sent three trusted men on what could have been a wild goose chase. Peter agreed to travel with three strangers to a gentile Roman centurion's home, not only breaking long-held Jewish restrictions but also doing something that would be seen by many Jews as consorting with their enemy military occupiers.

A key lesson is that we can expect what may seem like strange commands as we engage with God in his mission to reconcile

2. Doyle and Webster, *Dreams and Visions*.
3. J. Dudley Woodberry, Russell G. Shubin, and G. Marks, "Why Muslims Follow Jesus," *Christianity Today*, October 24, 2007, https://www.christianitytoday.com/ct/2007/october/42.80.html.

the world to himself. Cornelius is often considered to be the first gentile convert.[4] Whether or not that is true, his conversion marks a significant crossing of the Jew-gentile border in a gentile city and in the ministry of the apostle Peter, the leader of the Twelve.[5] Cornelius's conversion is the floodgate that opened the church to non-Jews. For most of us who lack any connection to the Jewish roots of Christianity, our own knowledge of Jesus as Lord and Savior can be traced back to the watershed moment of Cornelius's (or perhaps the Ethiopian eunuch's) conversion. But the significance of this conversion could only be appreciated in hindsight. Obeying God's commands to go where and to whom he directs may require us to give up our own assumptions of how, and in whom, God may be at work. But the rewards of such obedience are greater than we could ever ask or imagine.

The Spiritual Growth of Christians Who Share the Gospel

Another lesson arising from this conversion narrative is that evangelistic ministry not only results in the spiritual growth of converts but also transforms those who share the gospel. Peter's assumptions about how God works and who he might be calling were challenged by Cornelius's story. Peter learned something new about God. What new things about God might we learn by joining in his mission in this world that he loves so much?

Throughout its history, the church has been stretched to accept new peoples and new practices in order to reach out with the good news of Christ. Just as in the early church, when there was considerable controversy raised by the idea of welcoming gentiles into

4. Luke positions the Ethiopian eunuch's conversion as being *prior* to that of Cornelius, so it may well have been the eunuch who was the first gentile convert. However, since the eunuch's status as a possible Jewish proselyte has been discussed across the centuries, Cornelius's status as a more clearly recognized gentile likely led to him being labeled the first gentile convert.

5. F. F. Bruce, *The Book of the Acts*, New International Commentary on the New Testament (Grand Rapids: Eerdmans, 1988), 201.

the church of Christ, each new era has brought internal conflicts around questions of inclusion and exclusion. Consider just a few of the questions and controversies that have stretched the church. Should the Scriptures be translated into the languages of everyday people groups, or does that somehow alter the sanctity of Holy Scripture as rendered in the original languages? Should missionaries adopt local dress and cultural practices, or do such things blur the lines for people called to walk in a new path as followers of Christ? Answers to these questions seem obvious today, but those answers were far from obvious when they were first raised, as the church worried about the danger of syncretism and the erosion of clear boundaries. Faithful followers of Christ grappled with and fiercely debated such questions, growing through the process. As New Testament scholar Craig Keener points out, this reticence to embrace ethnically and culturally different newcomers is not a distinctively first-century Jewish problem but more generally a characteristic of all human beings. When believers from one culture evangelize people from another culture, they often fail to distinguish their own enculturation of the gospel from the gospel's transcultural story.[6]

The church continues to wrestle with certain issues arising in our own time. One such issue has arisen due to cross-cultural missionaries reporting that followers of Jesus now exist under the umbrella of other belief systems. Referred to as "insider movements," these are groups of people who begin to follow Jesus as Lord and Savior but continue to identify *culturally* as Muslims, Buddhists, or Hindus.[7] Such people are again stretching the church's understanding of whom God is calling, how he works, and what he requires of Christ followers.

For instance, does a person need to self-identify using the label "Christian" to be a follower of Christ? Many Christians today might answer, "Of course!" But the first followers of Christ didn't use this label, at least not initially. They continued to identify as

6. Keener, *Acts*, 2:1814.
7. Talman and Travis, *Understanding Insider Movements*.

faithful Jews and were first referred to as followers of "the Way," as six different references in the book of Acts show.[8] Nevertheless, their new faith in Christ required them to reshape their understanding of Jewish teachings, such as the role of the long-promised Jewish Messiah, the significance of sacrificial offerings, and the special and exclusive identity of Jews as the people of God. One such adaptation of Jewish practice shows up in this conversion narrative in the way Peter baptizes these new believers. Baptism, a common Jewish practice performed by both John's and Jesus's disciples, is now performed by Peter "in the name of Jesus Christ" (10:48).

Might God be continuing to stretch the church's understanding of both itself and the lordship of Christ through today's insider movements? Could the lordship of Christ supersede our familiar parameters? Issues of concern to the church, especially around orthodoxy, increase as the differences between belief systems increase. It is much easier to conceive of a follower of Christ who still identifies as a Jew (as today's Messianic Jews do) than it is to conceive of a follower of Christ who still identifies culturally as a Hindu or Buddhist. Just as Muslim-born believers come to know and revere Jesus as Lord and Savior rather than as simply a prophet, insider movements within these and other belief systems need to modify or even jettison many of their key beliefs about God and our relationship to him. How could such changes happen? Perhaps we'll only know the answer in hindsight in the decades and centuries ahead. However, one thing seems clear: the unrelenting God who welcomed Cornelius into his fold continues to surprise and stretch his church as he draws new people to himself.

The Christians who witnessed Cornelius's conversion grew in their own faith through the encouragement and joy that resulted from being part of God's work. For it was not only Cornelius and the other converts that day who experienced God in a new way. So too did Peter and the followers of Jesus who set out with him

8. Acts 9:2; 19:9, 23; 22:4; 24:14, 22.

from Joppa. By obeying God's command to venture into new territory, they received a powerful reminder of God's expansive love, perseverance, faithfulness, creativity, and power.

Later, other Christian leaders in Jerusalem also grew in their understanding of the expansiveness of God's grace when Peter told them what had happened in Cornelius's home (see Acts 11:1–18). While they were initially skeptical and angry about Peter entering a gentile household, they later rejoiced when he told the story of how the Holy Spirit had been poured out that day. In short, the course of the early church was deeply shaped by Cornelius's conversion because it didn't follow the normal process of conversion to Judaism, which required circumcision.[9]

The Inherently Missional Nature of Conversion

A final lesson to be drawn from this story is that conversion is inherently missional. Although in the West today, perhaps again due to influences of the Enlightenment, we have come to think of faith as a private matter and an individual and personal decision, this has not always been the case. The conversion of kings and chiefs often includes the conversion of their subjects and tribespeople. Cornelius the centurion's conversion was naturally accompanied by that of his household and others close to him.

The transformation of a new convert's life remains one of the most powerful forms of witness, since they are often already well-connected to other non-Christians. As in the case of Cornelius, the sacrament of baptism can provide an important witness to family, friends, neighbors, and colleagues as they consider why this person whom they know and love would be taking what they might consider to be a strange step. The commitment of the convert, demonstrated in the ministry of word and sacrament, carries missional potential for others. Therefore, it is important for churches to shape baptismal services with visitors in mind, encouraging those being baptized to invite their non-Christian friends

9. Keener, *Acts*, 2:1729.

and family, acknowledging and welcoming them, explaining what is occurring, including a word of personal witness from the new convert, and intentionally offering ways for seekers or the curious to explore the Christian faith for themselves.

In summary, the remarkable story of Cornelius's conversion, which takes place in the ancient, pluralistic Greco-Roman world, is rich in lessons for Christians hoping to reach new people within our own pluralistic Western world. This story reminds us about the preexisting spiritual lives of those we hope to reach, God's prevenient grace, God's role as the primary Evangelist, the extraordinary mystical phenomena he uses, the attentive obedience required of both evangelist and seeker, the growth that occurs in us when we share the gospel, and the inherently missional nature of conversion.

DISCUSSION QUESTIONS

1. Did you learn something new about God through the story of Cornelius's conversion?
2. In what ways do you think God was at work prior to you becoming a Christian?
3. Who obeyed God so that you could learn about Jesus?
4. Have you ever shared your faith with someone who wasn't a Christian? If so, what did you learn about God through that experience?

5

The Conversion of a
Desperate General

Naaman, commander of the army of the king of Aram, was a great man and in high favor with his master because by him the LORD had given victory to Aram. The man, though a mighty warrior, suffered from a skin disease. Now the Arameans on one of their raids had taken a young girl captive from the land of Israel, and she served Naaman's wife. She said to her mistress, "If only my lord were with the prophet who is in Samaria! He would cure him of his skin disease." So Naaman went in and told his lord just what the girl from the land of Israel had said. And the king of Aram said, "Go, then, and I will send along a letter to the king of Israel."

He went, taking with him ten talents of silver, six thousand shekels of gold, and ten sets of garments. He brought the letter to the king of Israel, which read, "When this letter reaches you, know that I have sent to you my servant Naaman, that you may cure him of his skin disease." When the king of Israel read the letter, he tore his clothes and said, "Am I God, to give death or life, that this man sends word to me to cure a man of his skin disease? Just look and see how he is trying to pick a quarrel with me."

But when Elisha the man of God heard that the king of Israel had torn his clothes, he sent a message to the king, "Why have you torn your clothes? Let him come to me, that he may learn that there is a prophet in Israel." So Naaman came with his horses and chariots and halted at the entrance of Elisha's house. Elisha sent a messenger to him, saying, "Go, wash in the Jordan seven times, and your flesh shall be restored, and you shall be clean." But Naaman became angry and went away, saying, "I thought that for me he would surely come out and stand and call on the name of the LORD his God and would wave his hand over the spot and cure the skin disease! Are not Abana and Pharpar, the rivers of Damascus, better than all the waters of Israel? Could I not wash in them and be clean?" He turned and went away in a rage. But his servants approached and said to him, "Father, if the prophet had commanded you to do something difficult, would you not have done it? How much more, when all he said to you was, 'Wash, and be clean'?" So he went down and immersed himself seven times in the Jordan, according to the word of the man of God; his flesh was restored like the flesh of a young boy, and he was clean.

Then he returned to the man of God, he and all his company; he came and stood before him and said, "Now I know that there is no God in all the earth except in Israel; please accept a present from your servant." But he said, "As the LORD lives, whom I serve, I will accept nothing!" He urged him to accept, but he refused. Then Naaman said, "If not, please let two mule loads of earth be given to your servant, for your servant will no longer offer burnt offering or sacrifice to any god except the LORD. But may the LORD pardon your servant on one count: when my master goes into the house of Rimmon to worship there, leaning on my arm, and I bow down in the house of Rimmon, when I do bow down in the house of Rimmon, may the LORD pardon your servant on this one count." He said to him, "Go in peace."

But when Naaman had gone from him a short distance, Gehazi, the servant of Elisha the man of God, thought, "My master has let that Aramean Naaman off too lightly by not accepting from him what he offered. As the LORD lives, I will run after him and get something from him." So Gehazi went after Naaman. When Naaman saw someone running after him, he jumped down from the chariot to meet him and said, "Is everything all right?" He replied, "Yes, but my master has sent me to say, 'Two members of a company of prophets have just come to me from the hill country of Ephraim;

please give them a talent of silver and two changes of clothing.'" Naaman said, "Please accept two talents." He urged him and tied up two talents of silver in two bags, with two changes of clothing, and gave them to two of his servants, who carried them in front of Gehazi. When he came to the citadel, he took the bags from them and stored them inside; he dismissed the men, and they left.

He went in and stood before his master, and Elisha said to him, "Where have you been, Gehazi?" He answered, "Your servant has not gone anywhere at all." But he said to him, "Did I not go with you in spirit when someone left his chariot to meet you? Is this a time to accept silver and to accept clothing, olive orchards and vineyards, sheep and oxen, and male and female slaves? Therefore the skin disease of Naaman shall cling to you and to your descendants forever." So he left his presence diseased, as white as snow.

—2 Kings 5:1–27

Why share the faith? This seems like a simple question with a simple answer: "Because Jesus told us to" or "Because the gospel is true." But given the dismal rate at which most Christians in the West are sharing the faith today, one wonders how the church really understands such answers or even the question itself. Many Christians seem to have little conviction that Jesus has told *them* to share the faith, and we seem to lack real conviction that the truth of Christianity has changed our own lives or that this truth could change our neighbors' or friends' lives or the life of the world.

This story of an ancient general's journey to faith in the living God holds up to the light the conviction, held by a number of people in the story, that by sharing what they know about God they could participate in God's work in Naaman's life and in the world. Before we get to that, however, let's first consider how this story points to the endemic problem of human suffering brought about by such things as illness, unhealthy pride, war, bigotry, and greed. For these, too, are issues the living God addresses in this story of conversion.

One Man's Very Human Pain

We are told that a great warrior, a commander of the army who was held in high favor by the king of Aram (Syria), suffered from a debilitating skin disease.[1] We don't know his exact condition, since the Hebrew word suggests symptoms associated with a number of skin ailments, one of which is Hansen's disease, also known as leprosy. We don't know exactly how Naaman was affected, but we know that, across the ages, illness has carried stigma with it, and in the ancient world skin diseases were particularly associated with a curse or judgment from the gods.[2]

The fact that this great general sought help from a foreign nation's prophet suggests his ailment significantly impacted his life. The severity of his condition is further suggested by the king of Aram writing a letter requesting help from the king of Israel. Since these two nations had often been at war, this would have been an extraordinary request. Finally, given that the skin is the largest organ of the body and protects us from a host of infections, any widespread disease of the skin could have serious physical consequences in the preantibiotic ancient world.

Beyond the physical consequences of skin diseases, there are also social consequences. Naaman's ailment may have affected his interactions with those under his authority in the Aramean army. It may have affected his relationships with the members of his household, including his wife. The story leaves us guessing at these things. The passage does tell us that the suffering of Naaman was sufficient enough for a powerless slave girl in his household to have known about the disease and to be moved to offer a small glimmer of hope.

Besides the skin disease, this great general had another sort of disease: a pride and privilege that almost cost him the chance to be healed. His powerful position, his grand entourage, and the

1. Although the Hebrew word is sometimes translated as "leprosy," scholars understand it to be broader in application, meaning "lesions" or "scaly skin," symptoms of a variety of skin diseases. Walton, Matthews, and Chavalas, *IVP Bible Background Commentary*, at 2 Kings 5:1–27.

2. Walton, Matthews, and Chavalas, *IVP Bible Background Commentary*, at 2 Kings 5:1–27.

immense wealth of money and items he brought with him as a gift evidently caused him to make assumptions about how he would be received and treated by the prophet Elisha.[3] He assumed he would be honorably greeted by the prophet. He assumed that the prophet would perform some grand ritual or incantation of healing over him. When these assumptions were not met, Naaman's position, power, and pride (even his pride in the great rivers of his homeland) nearly made him refuse the very simple instruction to "wash in the Jordan seven times" (5:10). It was his servants who convinced him to set aside his pride. And it was the servants who, every step of the way, served as catalysts in Naaman's transformation as God drew him to himself.

A Human War Prize

Let us turn to the character who first sets things in motion, the Israelite slave girl. Debilitating as this Syrian general's pride and illness were, he is not the only one suffering in this story. There is a collective brokenness evident in the story that still plagues the world: the human cost of military aggression. At the heart of the story is a girl from Samaria who was taken captive during one of the Aramean raids into Israel. We aren't told what physical or emotional scars she bore from this experience, but we know that such trauma is deep and long lasting.

We don't know how old she was when she was taken from her home and family. We don't even know her name. What we do know is that she remembered one key thing about her homeland. She remembered that there was a prophet in Samaria, and she had faith in that prophet's ability to cure her Aramean master's skin disease. This girl had faith in the healing power and love of God, and perhaps strangely, she wanted her Syrian master to experience this power and love.

3. The *IVP Bible Background Commentary* notes that in today's buying power, the silver and gold alone would be worth approximately three-quarters of a *billion* dollars. Walton, Matthews, and Chavalas, *IVP Bible Background Commentary*, at 2 Kings 5:1–27.

Political and Military Power

A third form of human brokenness is seen in the sparring between the kings of two nations, who had evidently been at odds before. The king of Aram sent Naaman with a personal letter to the king of Israel, instructing him to "cure him of his skin disease" (5:6). The king of Israel, no doubt due to the existing bad blood between them, saw this letter as a provocation, a reason for the king of Aram "to pick a quarrel" (v. 7). His focus was certainly more on the assumed political and military posturing of a rival king than it was on the suffering of the general who stood before him. This sad prioritization of political power over human well-being has been seen across the eons, as the sparring of powerful military and political opponents has resulted in untold suffering for those under their authority.

Human Prejudices, Jealousy, and Greed

Finally, we see one more kind of human brokenness in the figure of Gehazi, Elisha's servant who is the only one to be chastised in this story. Gehazi saw Naaman not as a fellow human being who had been encountered by the living God but as "that Aramean Naaman" who his master has let off "too lightly" (v. 20). We don't know exactly what lay at the root of Gehazi's disdain for Naaman. Perhaps it was simply that Naaman was an Aramean, a member of another ethnic group that was often a foe of Israel. Perhaps Gehazi or his loved ones had been affected by the Aramean raids into his country. Or perhaps he was simply jealous of Naaman's immense wealth. Whatever the reason, Gehazi's bigotry was shown in his plan to personally benefit from Naaman's healing and his gratefulness for that healing. Gehazi's sins of bigotry and greed were further evident when he lied to Elisha about his interaction with Naaman.

The story of Naaman's conversion points clearly to human suffering, brokenness, and sin within the human condition. Yet we see that God intended to address all of this brokenness. God seeks his shalom, the deep peace of well-being, for all of humanity. It was this shalom that Naaman discovered! His wonderment and gratefulness upon encountering the healing power of the God of Israel was palpable. We can picture him emerging from his seventh dunk in the Jordan and realizing his skin disease is gone. He had been touched by the God who saw his pain and made him whole in body, mind, and soul. His disease was gone, as were his unhealthy pride and sense of privilege.

Naaman recognized the hallowedness of the site where God had poured out his healing power, and he asked to take some soil from that place back with him. He wanted to make an altar where he could offer sacrifices to the Lord. He sought counsel from Elisha about how to navigate his role as the king of Aram's trusted general now that he knew and wanted to serve the God of Israel. He had been changed and would continue to be changed as he began worshiping and journeying with the Lord. So, what can we Christians, living thousands of years later and in a completely different culture, learn about evangelism, conversion, and discipleship from this story?

Be Willing to Be an Unlikely Evangelist

Consider the slave girl in this story. There is no evidence that she possessed any of the traits we often consider essential to being an evangelist. She likely had little education and may well have been illiterate. She may have never even spoken directly to Naaman herself, since that would have been highly unusual for a slave girl in that culture. She had a small sphere of influence as a child servant to Naaman's wife. Yet she used this sphere of influence to set off a chain of events that would result in this man of great influence and power being healed by the living God.

She was an unlikely evangelist in that she didn't answer philosophical questions or quote chapter and verse from the Scriptures. There is no evidence that she was a brilliant communicator or an extroverted street preacher. It's unlikely she would have made a great podcast host. Most of our images for an evangelist don't

73

really apply to her. And yet she brilliantly spoke a word of hope to someone when they needed to hear it. It may even have been an off-the-cuff remark as she mused about her former life in Samaria. All she did was share what she remembered and believed. But God made it enough.

Perhaps the most important thing for Christians to do is to believe that their small word of witness can be enough in the hands of God. Maybe this is just the sort of thing that Jesus was talking about when he said that the kingdom of God was like a mustard seed that someone took and sowed in their field (Mark 4:31–33). This small seed can, by God's grace, grow into a tree that gives shelter to all the birds of the air.

What small mustard seeds of the kingdom can each of us plant each day? Such small acts of witness as letting a friend know we are part of a church or telling a neighbor with a sick parent that we'll pray for them (or drive them to a medical appointment) can be seeds of the kingdom. These seeds may take the form of inviting that new colleague at work to a book club at your home, a family to a movie night at your church, or your eccentric aunt to a discussion group exploring the earliest biographies of Jesus. Or perhaps you can explore those biographies with her one-on-one over tea. Or maybe you'll plant a gospel seed when, after a baseball game, you tell your grandson how you became a Christian or about that time God's presence was especially comforting or challenging for you. Then again, perhaps planting gospel seeds begins with you asking God to help you attend to, and speak a small word of hope into, the everyday challenging situations you become aware of around you. Above all, ask God to give you a heart for people's wholeness and well-being, just as this little slave girl had. Pray for God's shalom to be at work in their lives and for you to play some small role in helping that along.

God May Use Many People to Reach One Person

Though the slave girl started the action, she did not operate alone in facilitating Naaman's journey to God. Two powerful kings, Elisha, and Naaman's servants all played important roles. When we offer a word of witness to someone, we can trust that God is not necessarily using us alone. As we've already seen, God is the primary Evangelist in the conversion of the human heart. He prodded the slave girl's memory of the prophet. God even used the rather pathetic king of Israel, someone who was so distressed by the king of Aram's letter that Elisha heard about it and sent the all-important message for Naaman to come to him. God also gave Naaman's servants the extraordinary courage to speak a word of encouragement at just the right time to their enraged and proud master.

In this story it is the supposedly powerless who end up exerting the most power over this Syrian general. The slave girl shared what she knew about the prophet Elisha; Elisha sent his servant to instruct Naaman in how to get healed in the river; and Naaman's own servants encouraged him to follow those simple instructions. God turned the tables on worldly power, using the meek to lead the great. Worldly power, embodied in Naaman and the two kings, was shown to be helpless, while faith, embodied in the slave girl, Naaman's servants, and Elisha, was shown to be triumphant.

Whether Large or Small, Use *Your* Sphere of Influence

The people who seem to have a huge sphere of influence (Naaman and the two kings) are not the people driving the action in this conversion story. It is those with small spheres of influence that count. We need to attend more to the small spheres of influence that each of us have with our kids, grandkids, cousins, nieces or nephews, a longtime friend, a new neighbor, or a colleague at work. Some of us will, of course, have a larger platform and may be able to share a word of witness within that sphere. But it seems that in the conversion stories of Scripture, a larger sphere is more rare (e.g., Peter preaching to the crowd that gathered on the feast of Pentecost). The normal context for effective evangelism was often one-on-one or small group conversations.

Imagine if every Christian today were to disciple just one person in their own sphere of influence during the next year. What we need now is for everyone with small spheres of influence to be willing to offer hurting people words of hope. We don't need more brilliantly gifted communicators and apologists. We need all of us. Maybe such a dream starts with some new prayers. I believe the words of Jesus have never been truer in this regard: "The harvest is plentiful, but the laborers are few; therefore ask the Lord of the harvest to send out laborers into his harvest" (Matt. 9:37).

Be Amazed at the Breadth of God's Grace

The most curious part of Naaman's story of conversion is his interaction with Elisha *after* his extraordinary healing, spiritual transformation, and expression of faith in the living God of Israel. Naaman quickly realized that his newfound faith was going to impact his everyday life in some important ways, and he asked Elisha to pardon him for one part of his job as an Aramean general: accompanying the Syrian king into the temple of Rimmon and bowing there (5:18–19).

Scholars tell us that this temple was likely the one built in Damascus to honor the leading god of the Syrians of that time, the god of storms, Hadad.[4] To be clear, to bow down in the temple of Rimmon, whether accompanying the king or not, would be seen as an act of worship. How could Naaman reconcile this act with his experience of and allegiance to the God of Israel? He asked Elisha for a pardon for this act, and he received it. All that Elisha said in response was, "Go in peace" (5:18).

While Elisha offered no explanation for this granting of grace to Naaman, it was surely a sign of God's expansive grace to this man whose conversion would no doubt affect those within his considerable sphere of influence. The people in his sizable entourage had already witnessed God powerfully transform their master's life. Now Naaman, commander of the Aramean army, would return to Syria where, on the Israeli soil he brought back with him, he would

4. Walton, Matthews, and Chavalas, *IVP Bible Background Commentary*, at 2 Kings 5:1–27.

offer sacrifices to the God of Israel. His accompaniment of the king into a foreign god's "house" and his actions there appeared to be of little interest to Elisha. To Elisha these would have been empty actions in a setting empty of spiritual significance. In no way was a Syrian idol a threat to the God of Israel. Naaman had been healed (in both body and soul) by the living God. He bore on his body a daily reminder of the power and love of God, and perhaps Elisha realized there could be no stronger testament of witness to the God of Israel than this healed general being physically present in the temple of Rimmon.

The people who God is calling to himself face real-life dilemmas as they learn to live into a new relationship with God and his people, and thus learn a new way of life. They have choices and accommodations to make as they interact with their friends, relatives, neighbors, colleagues, and broader culture. As more unchurched and dechurched adult converts come to faith, the church will need to learn to express the same grace shown by the prophet Elisha on that day so long ago on the shores of the Jordan River.

Be Careful of Your Motives

The only figure to be chastised in this conversion story is Gehazi, a servant of the prophet Elisha. His role as Elisha's servant, together with his daily proximity to Elisha, makes him the ultimate insider. He should know God and know God's ways. He should be familiar with God's lavish grace and God's power to transform people's lives. As someone who witnessed the humility required of Naaman when he was told to wash in the Jordan River, Gehazi should himself have been humbled and filled with wonderment and joy at Naaman's healing. But Gehazi was none of these things. Instead, he was consumed by the idea that he should profit from the Aramean general's extraordinary wealth.

Gehazi represents a warning to us as we engage in God's work of calling people to himself. Gehazi represents some possible ulterior motives that can underly our own engagement in evangelism. Is our motive the desire for our own ministry to be successful (i.e., greater numbers in our church)? Could the people we assume we are called to share the gospel with reveal our own underlying bigotry against or even fear of other people or people groups? Would we prefer to join in God's work only in the lives of people from our own class, ethnic group, or religious background? Are we tempted to sign up the wealthy as church members, hoping they will be part of the solution to a stretched church budget? God's judgment of Gehazi should serve as an important warning to us. May we continually examine our motives both individually and collectively. As we move out to share our faith, may we be compelled to do so by a vision of the kingdom of God that seeks the reconciliation of the *whole* world through Jesus Christ our Lord.

Let's examine now some of the compelling reasons to share the faith.

Biblical Warrant for Sharing the Faith

Naaman's conversion story is only one Old Testament example of God's mighty deeds to address human suffering and brokenness. The *missio Dei*, God's mission to reconcile the world to himself, is at the heart of the entire biblical narrative. In the Abrahamic blessing (Gen. 12:1–3; 28:14), God tells Abraham that he and his descendants will be a blessing to all nations. God's grace and presence extended to those who were considered outside the fold of Israel, as seen in the stories of such biblical figures as Melchizedek (Gen. 14), Jethro the Midianite, father-in-law of Moses (Exod. 18), Caleb and Othniel, the Canaanites (Num. 32:12; Judg. 3:9), Ruth the Moabite woman, the widow of Zarephath (1 Kings 17), and the people of Nineveh (Jon. 3). Additionally, both the prophet Isaiah and the prophet Zechariah refer to people of "the nations" who will follow Yahweh in ages to come (Isa. 2, 19, and Zech. 8).

In the New Testament Jesus sends out the seventy-two disciples to share the good news of God's peace and God's kingdom come near (Luke 10:1–16). This number, recorded as seventy in some manuscripts, represents all the known nations in the first century.

After the Lord's resurrection he again sends out his followers to make disciples, baptizing them and teaching them the good news under his authority, reminding them that he will be with them as they do so (Matt. 28:18–20). We read in Acts about Jesus's post-resurrection promise that his followers "will receive power when the Holy Spirit has come upon you, and you will be my witnesses in Jerusalem, in all Judea and Samaria, and to the ends of the earth" (Acts 1:8).

These texts from both the Old and New Testaments, and the biblical narrative as a whole, form the biblical warrant for evangelism. To be people who honor God's written Word, we need to take seriously the command to serve God in this world he loves by joining in his work of reconciling the whole created order to himself. As we read in Colossians 1,

> He is the image of the invisible God, the firstborn of all creation, for in him all things in heaven and on earth were created, things visible and invisible, whether thrones or dominions or rulers or powers—all things have been created through him and for him. He himself is before all things, and in him all things hold together. He is the head of the body, the church; he is the beginning, the firstborn from the dead, so that he might come to have first place in everything. For in him all the fullness of God was pleased to dwell, and through him God was pleased to reconcile to himself all things, whether on earth or in heaven, by making peace through the blood of his cross. (Col. 1:15–20)

Theological Warrant for Sharing the Faith

Flowing out from the biblical warrant for evangelism is a deeply theological warrant, as the very character of the triune God is focused on calling and sending in order that God's mission of salvation and reconciliation can be fully realized. In one of his post-resurrection narratives, John records Jesus telling his disciples, "Peace be with you. As the Father has sent me, so I send you" (John 20:21). This is crucial to remember as we join in the work of evangelism. It is in the very nature of God—Father, Son, and Holy Spirit—to call and send.

We see this theological grounding of mission in one of Paul's letters to the early church about Christians being given the role of ambassadors for Christ. Here too evangelism is not grounded in ourselves but in the very nature of God. Paul writes,

> So if anyone is in Christ, there is a new creation: everything old has passed away; look, new things have come into being! All this is from God, who reconciled us to himself through Christ and has given us the ministry of reconciliation; that is, in Christ God was reconciling the world to himself, not counting their trespasses against them, and entrusting the message of reconciliation to us. So we are ambassadors for Christ, since God is making his appeal through us; we entreat you on behalf of Christ: be reconciled to God. For our sake God made the one who knew no sin to be sin, so that in him we might become the righteousness of God. (2 Cor. 5:17–21)

Ecclesiological Warrant for Sharing the Faith

Paul's reminder that Christians serve as Christ's ambassadors to the nations leads naturally to a third warrant for evangelism: the call of the church grows out of God's own nature, as revealed to us in Scripture. This understanding of the church's missional identity can be seen in such historic documents as the Nicene Creed. First adopted by the church at the Council of Nicaea in AD 325, and slightly revised in AD 381, this creed offers one of the clearest and most memorable statements of what the church is: "We believe in one, holy, catholic, and apostolic Church." This short sentence contains the ideals that the church seeks to live out: unity, holiness, including people across time and cultures, and rootedness in the teaching and witness of the first apostles. A closer consideration of the word "apostolic" is instructive for our consideration of evangelism. What does the word "apostle" mean? Based on two Greek words, *apo* ("out") and *stellein* ("sent as an emissary"), it points to the church's vocation as being "sent out with a message." Mission is not simply one of many things the church is to do. Participating in the *missio Dei* is at the very heart of the church's identity.

Anthropological Warrant for Sharing the Faith

Finally, we come to the anthropological warrant for evangelism: the brokenness and sin endemic in the human condition. We see it all around us every day in the form of military atrocities, economic inequality, random acts of violence, broken and toxic relationships, heartbreaking identity crises, marginalization or exploitation of people and people groups, and disastrous environmental damage. These things are not new. Rather, they are as old as humanity itself. Paul, in writing to the church in Galatia, notes that the "works of the flesh" are easily recognized by all:

> Now the works of the flesh are obvious: sexual immorality, impurity, debauchery, idolatry, sorcery, enmities, strife, jealousy, anger, quarrels, dissensions, factions, envy, drunkenness, carousing, and things like these. I am warning you, as I warned you before: those who do such things will not inherit the kingdom of God. (Gal. 5:19–21)

This human predicament, of being separated from a holy God by our unholy sin, is perhaps best described in the heartbreaking story recorded in Genesis 3. In this story of the fall, we see four types of alienation resulting from human beings asserting their independence from their Creator. The first of these is their alienation from God, as the deep and life-giving relationship they had known was fractured by shame and fear. As the text says, "They heard the sound of the LORD God walking in the garden at the time of the evening breeze, and the man and his wife hid themselves from the presence of the LORD God among the trees of the garden" (3:8). People, although sensing the presence of God, have been hiding from God ever since.

The second form of alienation mentioned in the Genesis story is alienation from the self, as Adam and Eve felt ashamed of their own bodies for the first time. And surely this shame extended beyond their physical selves. They knew they had done wrong. They had claimed for themselves the right to be the judges of good and evil, eating the fruit from the tree of the knowledge of good and evil. Rather than looking to and depending on God, the maker of reality, to help them discern right from wrong, they asserted their moral independence. This would have catastrophic results for their sense of self, their relationships with others, and their relationship with creation.

The third form of alienation characteristic of the human condition is that of alienation from one another. Today, we are surrounded by gang warfare, domestic abuse, workplace rivalries, ethnic cleansings, nation battling nation, divorce, elder abuse, mass shootings, and the child sex trade. Adam blamed Eve, Eve blamed the serpent, and the blaming and shaming was passed on to the next generation as Cain killed Abel and interpersonal, clan, and national relationships spiraled downward.

The last form of alienation contained in Genesis 3 is that of alienation from creation. One result of the fall was that creation itself was cursed, making life a struggle for Adam. Fruitful abundance was replaced by scarcity and hardship. "By the sweat of your face you shall eat bread" (3:19). This situation has only spiraled downward, as humanity has exploited nature with little regard for either its renewal or God's shalom in the physical world around them.

These biblical, theological, ecclesiological, and anthropological warrants for evangelism should be taught in our churches regularly. A clear and compelling call for Christians to share this good news is needed so that those around us can hear a word of hope and a way out of the alienation that is part of human existence.

Why Share the Faith?

Across the ages there have been Christians who have felt compelled to tell others the good news of God reconciling the world in Christ because of the sheer beauty, grandeur, hopefulness, and joy of that metanarrative. Many others have felt compelled to tell others the good news because they have palpably experienced reconciliation with God. Some have found forgiveness for some dreadful thing they did years ago. For others, God has given them new meaning and a sense of purpose in life. For some, conversion has brought correction, direction, comfort, or a new sense of identity. And for others, knowing God has brought healing in body, mind, or soul. Many people have experienced a combination of these benefits. These small bits of good news, which flow from the broader good news, reveal that sharing the Christian faith changes lives and alters the course of history. This is the claim at the heart of Christianity: in Christ, God is reconciling the world to himself. By sharing the faith, we join in that great mission of God.

DISCUSSION QUESTIONS

1. What do you think compelled whoever it was who first shared the faith with you?
2. Of the biblical, theological, ecclesiological, and anthropological warrants for evangelism, which do you find the most compelling?
3. In what way do you think people can be "lost" if they don't yet know Jesus Christ?

6

The Conversion of a Prison Warden

One day as we were going to the place of prayer, we met a female slave who had a spirit of divination and brought her owners a great deal of money by fortune-telling. While she followed Paul and us, she would cry out, "These men are slaves of the Most High God, who proclaim to you the way of salvation." She kept doing this for many days. But Paul, very much annoyed, turned and said to the spirit, "I order you in the name of Jesus Christ to come out of her." And it came out that very hour.

But when her owners saw that their hope of making money was gone, they seized Paul and Silas and dragged them into the marketplace before the authorities. When they had brought them before the magistrates, they said, "These men, these Jews, are disturbing our city and are advocating customs that are not lawful for us, being Romans, to adopt or observe." The crowd joined in attacking them, and the magistrates had them stripped of their clothing and ordered them to be beaten with rods. After they had given them a severe flogging, they threw them into prison and ordered the jailer to keep them securely. Following these instructions, he put them in the innermost cell and fastened their feet in the stocks.

About midnight Paul and Silas were praying and singing hymns to God, and the prisoners were listening to them. Suddenly there was an earthquake so violent that the foundations of the prison were shaken, and immediately all the doors were opened and everyone's chains were unfastened. When the jailer woke up and saw the prison doors wide open, he drew his sword and was about to kill himself, since he supposed that the prisoners had escaped. But Paul shouted in a loud voice, "Do not harm yourself, for we are all here." The jailer called for lights, and rushing in, he fell down trembling before Paul and Silas. Then he brought them outside and said, "Sirs, what must I do to be saved?" They answered, "Believe in the Lord Jesus, and you will be saved, you and your household." They spoke the word of the Lord to him and to all who were in his house. At the same hour of the night he took them and washed their wounds; then he and his entire family were baptized without delay. He brought them up into the house and set food before them, and he and his entire household rejoiced that he had become a believer in God.

—Acts 16:16–34

Christians often think of evangelism as a one-on-one, person-to-person activity. This is often the case, as we've seen with Philip sharing the gospel with the Ethiopian eunuch, Andrew telling Peter, and Philip telling Nathanael. But what if evangelism can also be done corporately? How might the normal practices of our communities of faith be used by God to reach new people? The biblical conversion story of Paul and Silas's jailer helps us begin to explore how evangelism relates to ecclesial practices.

But first, what exactly are ecclesial practices? Since the earliest days of the church, Christians have been meeting to do things together as they relate to one another and the world as the body of Christ. Acts 2 paints a wonderful picture of some of the key practices of the church as a people called together to live into a new identity:

They devoted themselves to the *apostles' teaching* and *fellowship*, to the *breaking of bread* and the *prayers*. . . . All who believed were together and had all things in common; they would sell their

86

possessions and goods and *distribute the proceeds to all, as any had need*. Day by day, as they spent much *time together in the temple*, they *broke bread at home* and ate their food with glad and generous hearts, *praising God* and having the goodwill of all the people. (Acts 2:42, 44–47)

The ecclesial practices noted in this passage include reading and studying the teachings of the first apostles, meeting together for meals and fellowship, pooling resources to meet the needs of the poor, and gathering for worship in the temple in Jerusalem. Additionally, we know from many other references in the book of Acts that Christians met together to pray, to baptize people, and to worship together on what became known as the Lord's Day, referring to the day of the week on which Jesus's resurrection occurred. We also know from Paul's letters to the early church that they gathered to remember the death of Jesus in a sacramental act known as the Lord's Supper, Holy Communion, or Eucharist.

Such a list of Christian communal practices is not surprising since the first Christians were Jews, and Judaism emphasizes communal practices in addition to individual ones. Whether gathering around family dinner tables for the Shabbat and Seder meals, or gathering at synagogues for celebration of holy days, these sorts of communal practices formed the foundation of ecclesial practices in the early church. Now we'll explore how such ecclesial practices are linked to evangelism in the story of the jailer's conversion.

Gathering Together

One of the first things to note in this story is that the opening paragraph includes many plural personal pronouns and other indicators that the Christians in this story are traveling together. The opening paragraph is peppered with such phrases as "*we were going* to the place of prayer," "*we met* a female slave," "while she followed *Paul and us*," and "*these men* are slaves of the Most High God." At their heart, shared ecclesial practices are just that: shared. This story, and so many like it, suggests that gathering and traveling together in pairs or small groups was the custom for Christians. In this narrative we see Christians *together*: in a place of prayer, in the marketplace, before the magistrates of that city, in a jail, and in a household.

Meeting together, as a basic practice of the church of Christ, is assumed throughout the New Testament. The various writers of the epistles wrote letters to churches gathered from their local communities, and these were often then circulated among churches in different communities. This gathering was a commanded practice that was to be lived out in mutual service, as Paul wrote to the Corinthians about what their life together was to look like. We also see in the letter to the Hebrews the following instruction: "And let us consider how to provoke one another to love and good deeds, not neglecting to meet together, as is the habit of some, but encouraging one another, and all the more as you see the Day approaching" (Heb. 10:24–25).

Praying Together

In this story of conversion, in which Christians were traveling and ministering together, we learn that praying together was also normative. They traveled *together* to a place of prayer. Once again, prayer *preceded* mighty missional acts of God, but this time prayer was offered corporately. Whether freeing a slave girl from a spirit of divination or providing a witness to prisoners, a jailer, and magistrates, when the church prays together, they are led into powerful witness for the gospel, and that witness brings transformative freedom, truth, and justice.

Proclaiming Together

Paul's public exorcism of a "spirit of divination" and his and Silas's speaking "the word of the Lord" to the jailer and his household are examples of public witness as a practice of the church. These encounters taught those who were directly addressed and observers alike about the power of God and the way of life that followers of Jesus Christ were called to. Unlike so much of the church's proclamation today, which is heavily focused on preaching to Christians, these proclamations were inherently missional. They occurred in public settings: in the marketplace, before the magistrates of the city, in the jail, and in the home of the jailer. The early church was less associated with buildings and more associated with a community of people that proclaimed a message of hope.

Suffering Together

This brings us to what is perhaps the most puzzling aspect of this conversion story: the brutal beating and imprisonment of Paul and Silas. Suffering is not something we like to think about. This is especially true when we consider how we ourselves might be called to suffer as members of the church. But across the ages of the church, and certainly in this story from the early church, suffering together for the sake of the gospel has been considered normative. This is described in Paul's instruction to Timothy as a junior pastor: "Do not be ashamed, then, of the testimony about our Lord or of me his prisoner, but *join with me in suffering for the gospel*, in the power of God" (2 Tim. 1:8).

This same exhortation is found throughout the New Testament. Consider Peter's encouragement, not written to an individual Christian but intended as a letter to be circulated among churches scattered throughout "Pontus, Galatia, Cappadocia, Asia, and Bithynia" (1 Pet. 1:1):

> Beloved, do not be surprised at the fiery ordeal that is taking place among you to test you, as though something strange were happening to you. But rejoice insofar as you are sharing Christ's sufferings, so that you may also be glad and shout for joy when his glory is revealed. If you are reviled for the name of Christ, you are blessed, because the spirit of glory, which is the Spirit of God, is resting on you. But let none of you suffer as a murderer, a thief, a criminal, or even as a mischief maker. Yet if any of you suffers as a Christian,

do not consider it a disgrace, but glorify God because you bear this name. (1 Pet. 4:12–16)

Similarly, in Acts the practice of being brought in and persecuted because of being identified as a Christ follower was considered an honor. As Luke writes of the apostles, "As they left the council, they rejoiced that they were considered worthy to suffer dishonor for the sake of the name" (5:41).

This view of suffering is not distinctive of the epistles alone; it is also found within the teachings of Jesus himself. In Matthew's Gospel account we read these words from Jesus's Sermon on the Mount: "Blessed are you when people revile you and persecute you and utter all kinds of evil against you falsely on my account" (Matt. 5:11). Similar encouragement is included in John's Gospel, as Jesus links the suffering of the church to his own suffering, saying to his gathered disciples, "Remember the word that I said to you, 'Slaves are not greater than their master.' If they persecuted me, they will persecute you; if they kept my word, they will keep yours also" (John 15:20). It is a somewhat unwelcome and threatening concept to much of the church in the West today, but it is clear that Jesus and his first disciples viewed the suffering of the Christian community as normative. And when they suffered, they often suffered together, as Paul and Silas did.

Making Music Together

Another ecclesial practice evident in this conversion story is that of singing hymns to God. Born out of Jewish practices of worship, the singing of hymns, especially the psalms, was a common practice of early Christian worship. The text tells us that it was midnight, and we are left to imagine the darkness of the innermost cell in which Paul and Silas were shackled following their beating. They were no doubt hurting, tired, and hungry. Yet they were singing, and the other prisoners were listening as Paul and Silas offered worship to God. It's important to note that their singing was *not* directed at their fellow prisoners but to God. Nevertheless, their worship was also witness: it was no doubt as strange then as it would be today for people in such dire circumstances to be making music together as an act of worship.

However, such behavior seems less strange when we think back to Paul's own admonition to the churches in Ephesus and Colossae. Paul contrasts worship of God with leading a life of meaningless self-gratification. Singing psalms, hymns, and spiritual songs is deeply connected to being both filled with the Holy Spirit and formed by the written word.

> Do not get drunk with wine, for that is debauchery, but be filled with the Spirit, as you sing psalms and hymns and spiritual songs to one another, singing and making melody to the Lord in your hearts. (Eph. 5:18–19)

> Let the word of Christ dwell in you richly; teach and admonish one another in all wisdom; and with gratitude in your hearts sing psalms, hymns, and spiritual songs to God. (Col. 3:16)

Paul and Silas were singing music not simply to lift their own spirits. They were practicing a key ecclesial practice of the early church: worshiping together.

Making Disciples Together

A sixth ecclesial practice seen in the conversion of the jailer is a communal focus on disciple-making. Experiencing an earthquake in the dead of night while shackled in an innermost cell must have been terrifying. But Paul and Silas remained focused on the well-being of others, which included sharing with them the good news of Christ. They called out to stop the jailer from taking his own life in an act of desperation. If his prisoners had escaped, he would have been held accountable as jail warden. If attributed to a dereliction of duty, this offense was often punishable by death, so his plan to take his own life was perhaps reasonable. Paul and Silas helped save the jailer's life, but they didn't stop there. They turned to saving his soul. Again, the plural pronoun is used repeatedly throughout this text. In short, they told him to believe in Jesus. The text reveals that "*they* spoke the word of the Lord to him *and to all who were in his house*" (Acts 16:32).

Sharing the Sacraments Together

One ecclesial practice leads to another. As with the conversion of the Ethiopian eunuch and Cornelius, the jailer was baptized after coming to Christ through the disciple-making ministry of the church. And as with Cornelius, the other members of the jailer's household were also baptized. This points again to the shared nature of belief and identity among households in the ancient world. The sacrament of baptism was shown to be a missional event when a person of influence, such as the head of a household, came to believe in Jesus and committed to following him.

Calling for Justice Together

Included in both the prologue and the final section of this conversion story, a final ecclesial practice is the church's action for truth and justice. Since Paul and Silas were Roman citizens, their detention, beating, and incarceration without trial was unlawful. The discovery of their Roman citizenship was particularly embarrassing, even horrifying, to the magistrates, since the city of Philippi was a Roman colony and thus a place where citizenship mattered greatly.[1] While they could have simply left quietly once they were released by the magistrates, they chose to stay in the jail until their unlawful imprisonment was acknowledged by the magistrates. Their principled stance showed that, as the church, they were interested in more than their personal freedom. They wanted their ill treatment to lead to truth-telling and to a correction to those imposing unjust legal processes and practices. They were prodding the system to change for the better.

1. Keener, *Acts*, 3:2382.

The Witness of the Church Being the Church

Having outlined how ecclesial practices are connected to the conversion of the jailer and his household in the first century, let us consider how the *shared life* of churches might be linked to evangelism and disciple-making in our own age. In his book *Evangelism after Christendom*, Bryan Stone notes the continued relevance of this question:

> Christian salvation is ecclesial—that its very shape in the world *is* a participation in Christ through the worship, shared practices, loyalties, and social patterns of his body, the church. To construe the message of the gospel in such a way as to hide or diminish the unique social creation of the Spirit that the first Christians called *ecclesia* is to miss the point of what God is up to in history—the calling forth and creation of a people. The most evangelistic thing the church can do, therefore, is to be the church not merely in public but as a new and alternative public; not merely in society but as a new and distinct society, a new and unprecedented social existence.[2]

Darrell Guder, in offering an incarnational model of evangelism, also writes of such a view of the church as an alternative society that bears witness by its very presence.[3] Guder connects the incarnation to the lived witness of the life of the church. Christ is the self-emptying servant, born into the human family, living among his creation, giving his life on the cross for them, and confirming his identity and victory in the resurrection. Similarly, the good news of the gospel is to be lived out—incarnated—in a particular place and time until the coming of the kingdom in its fullness. The focus of this good news is *God with us*. Love is dominant in both the what and how of the church's proclamation, as practices of the faith are lived out on the ground.

This model of evangelism can be seen across the ages of the church, but it is uniquely apparent in the life shared together by missional communities of Celtic monks in the fifth and sixth

2. Stone, *Evangelism after Christendom*, 15.
3. Guder, "Incarnation and the Church's Evangelistic Mission," 171–84.

centuries. In *The Celtic Way of Evangelism*, George Hunter describes key characteristics of the missionary work led by Patrick, who ministered to the celts of Ireland; Columba, who brought the gospel to the Picts of Scotland; and Aidan, who led the re-evangelization of the Anglo-Saxons in eastern England. One hallmark of Celtic Christian evangelism was the formation of apostolic teams made up of approximately a dozen people, including priests, laypeople, seminarians, and porters.[4] They first connected with the leaders of a new location, seeking permission to settle there, establishing contact with those in positions of influence and power and only then starting a community near the tribal settlement. These teams befriended the people, learning their language, culture, and worldview, first by listening and attending in order to find possible bridges between their culture and the gospel message.[5] These Celtic missionary groups sought to win the respect of the leaders and people of their new missionary location by modeling a Christ-centered life and by offering conversation, prayer, counsel, and meditation. It was only after people began to come to faith in Christ, to be baptized, and to receive the Eucharist that churches were built, with one of the apostolic team members being appointed as a priest and pastor to the new community.[6] The team would then move on to another location to plant the next church.

How effective were these apostolic teams in bringing the gospel to Ireland, Scotland, and eastern England? Hunter suggests that Patrick's teams alone "planted seven hundred churches and that Patrick ordained perhaps one thousand priests. Within his lifetime, 30 to 40 (or more) of Ireland's 150 tribes became substantially Christian."[7] One would think that the established leaders of the church in England would have been supportive of such evangelistic efforts. However, as Hunter outlines, "the British leaders were offended and angered that Patrick was spending priority time not

4. Hunter, *Celtic Way of Evangelism*, 9.
5. Hunter, *Celtic Way of Evangelism*, 8.
6. Hunter, *Celtic Way of Evangelism*, 10.
7. Hunter, *Celtic Way of Evangelism*, 11.

with church people but with pagans, sinners, and barbarians."[8] Hunter notes that such perspectives are not foreign to our own time:

> This perspective is astonishingly widespread today. Pastors and churches today who regard outreach to lost people as the church's main business, and especially those who are perceived to prefer the company of lost people to the company of church people, are suspect, marginalized, and "shot at" by establishment Christians and church leaders. No major denomination in the United States regards apostolic ministry to card-carrying, secular, pre-Christian outsiders as its priority or even as normal ministry.[9]

How might we change this situation? Could the church across North America and Europe today see small groups of Christians living out ecclesial practices as a distinct society for the purposes of both worshiping God and sharing the gospel with the people who surround them? What would this look like on the ground as Christians meet and practice life together? This will take any number of forms, each of which will require us to demonstrate countercultural practices in the broader culture.

Making Prayer for New Disciples a Priority

There are few churches that would not say prayer is a priority for them. But what is the focus of their prayers as they gather for worship or conduct business meetings or plan programming or discuss what outreach projects they plan to fund? Are evangelism and mission emphasized only during a special sermon series or on a special missions Sunday? Or are these included in the normative weekly prayer life of the church? When gathering for worship on Sunday is it a regular practice to pray that we will build authentic friendships with non-Christians so that the groundwork for sharing the gospel can be established? What would happen if every

8. Hunter, *Celtic Way of Evangelism*, 12.
9. Hunter, *Celtic Way of Evangelism*, 12–13.

single time church members gathered, they prayed for people who have spiritual questions and longings to come to know Christ? What if every church budget meeting started with a reminder that the church exists for two purposes: to worship God and to share the gospel with those around us? Let's infuse, into every single gathering of the church, prayers for the people in our neighborhoods who have spiritual questions and longings. Every choir or worship band practice, every worship service, every meeting of vestry or elders, every children's ministry planning meeting, every Bible study, and every outreach committee meeting. Let's pray together for new people to come to know Jesus.

Suffering for the Gospel

There is very little physical persecution happening in the lives of Christians in North America and Europe today. Most of us will live our whole lives without suffering for the gospel. Unlike our sisters and brothers in places such as Iran, Sudan, Nigeria, Pakistan, and parts of India, we don't worry that our children will be abducted from their schools and forced to convert to another faith. Our property won't be seized nor will our businesses or homes be burned simply because we are identified as Christian. We don't face potential imprisonment for sharing our faith with someone or because something we said was judged to be blasphemy.

Across North America and most of Europe, Christians live under laws guaranteeing protection of freedom of religion. We are granted a certain official recognition due to the residual effects of Christendom. For example, Canadians can claim as charitable donations the tithes and offerings given to the church, and there is still some public funding of many Christian religious schools. Christians remain the largest faith group across both Canada and the United States.

Nevertheless, the waning of Christendom has resulted in some serious and well-deserved critique of the church's alignment with colonialism, clergy sexual abuse of children, and the stigmatization and abuse of Indigenous peoples who chose to practice their traditional beliefs. Together with the rising percentage of North Americans who describe themselves as having no religion, such criticism of the church can feel threatening to Christians. Perhaps it's time to give up the last vestiges of Christendom and humbly embrace a willingness to admit past wrongs and to suffer for the sake of the gospel, even if that "suffering" now only means being the butt of an office joke, being passed over for a promotion, being wrongly associated with right-wing extremists, or being avoided socially. Are we willing to love our non-Christian neighbors, colleagues, and family even when some of them treat us like social lepers and freaks? Rather than becoming defensive and retreating into private Christian enclaves or dividing ourselves into publicly secular but privately spiritual beings, we must do the hard work of building trust, stimulating curiosity, engaging in meaningful discussion, answering questions, and discipling in the present climate, which is increasingly skeptical of the claims of Christianity.

Allowing Worship to Be a Witness

Just as Paul and Silas prayed and sang as they worshiped God within the walls of a first-century prison, perhaps it's time for Christians to be willing to worship outside the walls of church buildings. Some of this is already happening through things like the Fresh Expressions movement, which began during the 1990s in the UK, with the support of both the Church of England and the British Methodist Church. From this movement emerged a variety of new forms of worshiping together as the church. Messy Churches are engaging families with young children in worship involving crafts, singing, simple prayers, and a shared meal. Café churches are seeing people gather in coffee shops to read and discuss Scripture and pray together. Bakery churches are drawing in new people with an affinity for baking bread together while they build friendships, discuss the teachings of Jesus, learn about faith together, enjoy the delicious fruit of their labors, and pray for needs that arise in their discussion.

As this movement continues to spread across America, Canada, New Zealand, and Australia, other forms of being together as church have developed, with a particular focus on reaching new people with the gospel message. These include surfer church, goth church, night church, skateboard church, and dinner church. Wherever people come together over some sort of affinity, a new form of church can grow. Although most fresh expressions of church are small, these groups of Christians are reaching substantial numbers of new people with the gospel, in much the same way that Paul and Silas did.

Another way that worship can both be directed to God and be a missional witness is to open up established churches to allow more people to explore Christianity, even if only as observers. Churches can hold some services outdoors. They can open their doors and windows to allow people outside to listen to what is being sung. They can host worship services for special occasions, such as Veterans Day or Remembrance Day. They can host a neighborhood memorial service at the site of a tragic event in the community. They can hold baptism services at a local lake or river.

The Deeply Missional Effect of Baptism

As seen in the story of the jailer's conversion, baptism was a missional event, as an entire household was welcomed into the Christian faith. Even in our more individualistic society, baptism is an event rich with missional potential as non-Christian family, friends, colleagues, and neighbors attend such services to support the person being baptized. To hear a loved one make baptismal promises or give a public proclamation as to why they are taking this sacramental step is a powerful witness to those gathered for the event. Churches today should not miss the opportunity to extend their witness of the gospel as they acknowledge the powerful effect that baptism can have on those in attendance who are then touched by the call of God on their own lives.

Standing Together against Injustice

In the story of the conversion of Paul and Silas's jailer, followers of Jesus confront the local magistrates, who by lack of due process had ignored the lawful treatment of Roman citizens. To beat and imprison a person of Roman citizenship without a trial was a criminal offense.[10] This unjust suffering put Paul and Silas in a position of power that resulted in their public vindication. In their refusal to be further intimidated, they ignored the magistrates' pleas to leave Philippi immediately, instead meeting with believers gathered at Lydia's home prior to their departure. Paul, Silas, and their traveling companions were standing together for justice. Their actions, as well as Luke's recording of these particular events, highlight and challenge the systemic injustice committed by both the magistrates and the owners of the fortune teller slave girl. Such systemic change has long been part of the church's focus as it has striven to be a sign, foretaste, and instrument of the kingdom of God. At its best, the church has called for an end to slavery, more humane prison conditions, and better care for orphans and widows. Christians have worked together to adopt and raise abandoned babies. They have provided food and shelter for lepers and those affected by plague. They have worked to establish hospitals and schools. They have offered safe houses for victims of sex trafficking and provided burial for those who have died in refugee camps. The church at its best has called for kingdom-of-God values to be enacted in society, values that lead to human flourishing.

One thing is clear when looking across the world today: the gospel message needs to once again be proclaimed winsomely and clearly. It will take more than a few gifted evangelists. It is going to take churches that have come alive to the reality of a calling and sending God and have heard God's call to share the good news with the lost. This endeavor will involve many one-on-one evangelistic encounters, but it will also require churches to be incarnationally countercultural and share their life with the

10. Keener, *Acts*, 3:2517.

surrounding world. It will require unhuddled, courageous, and loving churches that understand the deep connections between their ecclesial practices and the sharing of the faith with people whom God is calling to himself.

DISCUSSION QUESTIONS

1. How do you think the jail warden's daily life changed following his conversion?
2. Which of the ecclesial practices seen in this story are emphasized in your present church: traveling out together for the sake of mission, praying for those outside the church, being willing to suffer persecution as a result of proclaiming the gospel, worshiping outside the church building, caring for those working or incarcerated in the prison system, baptizing new disciples of Jesus, and acting for truth and justice to be upheld?
3. What ecclesial practices can your church develop to introduce new people to Jesus?

7

The Conversion of a Child Prophet

Now the boy Samuel was ministering to the LORD under Eli. The word of the LORD was rare in those days; visions were not widespread.

At that time Eli, whose eyesight had begun to grow dim so that he could not see, was lying down in his room; the lamp of God had not yet gone out, and Samuel was lying down in the temple of the LORD, where the ark of God was. Then the LORD called, "Samuel! Samuel!" and he said, "Here I am!" and ran to Eli and said, "Here I am, for you called me." But he said, "I did not call; lie down again." So he went and lay down. The LORD called again, "Samuel!" Samuel got up and went to Eli and said, "Here I am, for you called me." But he said, "I did not call, my son; lie down again." Now Samuel did not yet know the LORD, and the word of the LORD had not yet been revealed to him. The LORD called Samuel again, a third time. And he got up and went to Eli and said, "Here I am, for you called me." Then Eli perceived that the LORD was calling the boy. Therefore Eli said to Samuel, "Go, lie down, and if he calls you, you shall say, 'Speak, LORD, for your servant is listening.'" So Samuel went and lay down in his place.

Now the LORD came and stood there, calling as before, "Samuel! Samuel!" And Samuel said, "Speak, for your servant is listening." Then the LORD said to Samuel, "See, I am about to do something in

Israel that will make both ears of anyone who hears of it tingle. On that day I will fulfill against Eli all that I have spoken concerning his house, from beginning to end. For I have told him that I am about to punish his house forever for the iniquity that he knew, because his sons were blaspheming God, and he did not restrain them. Therefore I swear to the house of Eli that the iniquity of Eli's house shall not be expiated by sacrifice or offering forever."

Samuel lay there until morning; then he opened the doors of the house of the Lord. Samuel was afraid to tell the vision to Eli. But Eli called Samuel and said, "Samuel, my son." He said, "Here I am." Eli said, "What was it that he told you? Do not hide it from me. May God do so to you and more also, if you hide anything from me of all that he told you." So Samuel told him everything and hid nothing from him. Then he said, "It is the Lord; let him do what seems good to him."

As Samuel grew up, the Lord was with him and let none of his words fall to the ground. And all Israel from Dan to Beer-sheba knew that Samuel was a trustworthy prophet of the Lord. The Lord continued to appear at Shiloh, for the Lord revealed himself to Samuel at Shiloh by the word of the Lord. And the word of Samuel came to all Israel.

—1 Samuel 3:1–4:1

The story of Samuel's conversion is one of the most beautiful yet strange stories of Scripture. Set in a time of transition between the period of the judges and the kings of Israel, this story unequivocally demonstrates that God calls children to know, trust, and serve him. Sometimes he does this using mystical experiences. It is a story that also points to the role of parents and elders who can nurture, encourage, and guide children in knowing and loving God. It is a story that unpacks the reciprocal and complex relationship between witness and vocation. And finally, this is a story that shows how a person of any age can be steeped in religion and yet not really know God. Let's begin by focusing on what this story teaches us about God.

102

God Knows Us

Although the story of Samuel's conversion is told in 1 Samuel 3, the first two chapters of this book give us some important backstory. In these chapters we learn about his parents, two people of deep faith and abiding obedience. God sees Elkanah bringing his family to offer sacrifices to God in the tabernacle at Shiloh year after year. God also sees Hannah, year after year, praying to have a child. God is clearly central to and active in the lives of not just individuals but also families such as Elkanah and Hannah's. Although we are told that "Samuel did not yet know the LORD" (3:7), God already knew this family well before Samuel was born. The faith of this couple stands in contrast to many others in their time, and Hannah's prayer affirms that "for the LORD is a God of knowledge, and by him actions are weighed" (2:3).[1]

God also knew the sorry state of Israel during this time. The last line of the book of Judges reminds us that "there was no king in Israel; all the people did what was right in their own eyes" (Judg. 21:25). People were ignoring God's law. There was corruption within the priesthood, as Eli's sons, Hophni and Phinehas, committed extortion and engaged in wicked sexual behavior. And parental authority had broken down, as Eli's warning to his sons fell on deaf ears, and he neglected to follow up with any real consequences. God saw and knew all of this.

God Speaks to Us

Throughout this story we see God speaking, either through the mouth of someone he sends as a prophet or through a direct revelation. First, God sent an unnamed "man of God" (2:27) to bring a prophetic word of judgment against Eli and his family. Next, God spoke to Samuel, a boy living and serving in the tabernacle. Samuel heard the voice and mistook it for that of Eli. But the text says

---

1. Hannah's full prayer is recorded in 1 Sam. 2:1–10.

that after receiving Eli's instruction, Samuel was given a vision in which "the LORD came and stood there, calling as before, 'Samuel! Samuel!'" (3:10). The Lord gave Samuel a message to convey to Eli as a witness to all Israel. It was a message of judgment against the evil being done and left unchecked within Eli's family.

God Calls and Equips Us

God's threefold nighttime calling of Samuel leads to his vocation as a prophet of God, a ministry he would carry out for the rest of his life. He learned that night that this vocation first required him to *listen* for God's word. He learned too that what he heard would not always be pleasant or easy to convey. But he would go on to speak God's word to God's people. Samuel's vocation as a prophet began that night in the tabernacle, but the preparation for that night was put in place by God long before.

The Key Role of Elkanah and Hannah

In ancient Judaism, parents were the primary spiritual educators of their children. Faith began at home. Several commands related to this are found in the book of Deuteronomy. These include such passages as Deuteronomy 4:9, which admonishes parents to first remember God's word spoken to them, "but take care and watch yourselves closely, so as neither to forget the things that your eyes have seen nor to let them slip from your mind all the days of your life; make them known to your children and your children's children."

This same command is reiterated in Deuteronomy 6:4–7:

Hear, O Israel: The LORD is our God, the LORD alone. You shall love the LORD your God with all your heart and with all your soul and with all your might. Keep these words that I am commanding you today in your heart. Recite them to your children and talk about them when you are at home and when you are away, when you lie down and when you rise.

This role of parents is further affirmed in the words of Psalm 78:4, which says,

> We will not hide them from their children;
> we will tell to the coming generation
> the glorious deeds of the LORD and his might
> and the wonders that he has done.

Samuel was brought to live at the tabernacle at Shiloh shortly after he was weaned. Hannah dedicated her son to the service of God, in thanks for his birth. Elkanah and Hannah continued to make their annual pilgrimage to Shiloh to offer their sacrifices and worship to God, with Hannah bringing her growing son Samuel a new robe each time she made her pilgrimage to Shiloh (1 Sam. 2:19–20). The story of his mother's initial infertility and the extraordinary circumstances of his conception were no doubt told to Samuel, just as they were recorded in the book that bears his name. Elkanah and Hannah were people of deep faith, reflected in their prayers for and committal of their firstborn to God's service. How this family's strong Jewish faith affected Samuel we can't be sure. But it was Hannah bringing him to live with Eli in the tabernacle at Shiloh that set the stage for Samuel's remarkable childhood encounter with God.

Eli's Flaws and Strengths

In contrast to Elkanah and Hannah, Eli is portrayed as a less-than-ideal father to his two sons. "They had no regard for the LORD" (1 Sam. 2:12), but they were still serving in the respected role of priests, abusing this role by coercing women coming to the tabernacle into giving them sexual favors and demanding the choice cuts of meat being offered as sacrifices to God. As the text records, "Thus the sin of the young men was very great in the sight of the LORD, for they treated the offerings of the LORD with contempt" (2:17). Although Eli had warned them against continuing their bad behavior, he had failed to remove them from their roles.

However, God in his grace gave Eli a second chance to influence a child for God, placing Samuel in his care. In 1 Samuel 3 we see a tired, old, and nearly blind Eli telling Samuel how to respond to God if he were to call to him a third time. It was Eli who instructed Samuel to say "Speak, for your servant is listening" (3:10), establishing the prophetic practice of first listening for the word of God. Eli then pressed Samuel to tell him the complete message that God gave him. This too would be key for Samuel's future ministry, as he would need to deliver some difficult words from God to Israel and its first kings. Finally, when Eli received the bad news of God's judgment on his family, he replied not with anger but with acceptance, saying, "It is the LORD; let him do what seems good to him" (3:18). In this response Eli provided a strong example to Samuel, whom he neither castigated nor even reprimanded for delivering this dark message. Eli no doubt failed his natural sons, but he provided a good example and guidance to his spiritual son, Samuel.

Witness and Vocation in the Metanarrative of God

This story demonstrates well that the relationship between witness and vocation is a self-replicating relationship. We see that Hannah's, Elkanah's, and Eli's witness to Samuel all played a role in his rise to the vocation of prophet. This in turn led to Samuel being a witness to others, including Eli, Saul, David, and all of Israel. Note especially that Samuel's vocation was not simply for him. By living into his vocation, he joined the grand narrative of God at work in God's world. The final verse of chapter 3 records, "The LORD revealed himself to Samuel at Shiloh by the word of the LORD" (3:21). Samuel's vocation as a prophet of God was predicated on God's own actions and teachings, reaching back across time and recorded in his word. Samuel's vocation was also instrumental for where God wanted to lead Israel in the future. Witness leads to discernment of vocation, and vocation leads to further witness, as God works out his grand narrative of redemption across the ages.

Samuel as a Child—Religious but Not Spiritual

Samuel's story is a reminder that the gospel needs to be shared with children both inside and outside the community of faith. This story is a corrective to those who assume that if a child is raised in the church, they necessarily have a living relationship with God. This simply isn't true.

In terms of location, Samuel could not have been closer to the center of Jewish religious practices. As the text notes, "The boy Samuel was ministering to the LORD under Eli" and "was lying down in the temple of the LORD, where the ark of God was" (3:1, 3). The "temple" in this verse was the tabernacle, the portable tent repeatedly set up and taken down during the Israelites' trek through the wilderness of Sinai; it was later set up at Shiloh after the Israelites settled in Canaan. It served as the central place of worship for over three centuries, until the building of the Jerusalem temple by Solomon. Since being weaned, likely around age two or three, Samuel had lived at the tabernacle, even sleeping in the tent that housed the holiest religious artifact of ancient Israel, the ark of God, which symbolized God's presence and power in their midst.

And yet the text tells us that "Samuel did not yet know the LORD, and the word of the LORD had not yet been revealed to him" (3:7). He was an Israelite living in the very center of these Jewish religious practices, with the various religious festivals, holy days, offerings, and rituals, but he did not yet know the God of Abraham, Isaac, and Jacob. Thus, the story of Samuel's conversion should be a cautionary one to parents and to the church as a whole. Children raised in church still need to be personally encountered by God. Such an encounter could make the difference between them either discovering or missing the life that God is calling them to.

Sharing Faith with Children in a Time of Unbelief

Isn't it fascinating that this story of a child's conversion begins with a reference to an age in which "the word of the LORD was rare" and "visions were not widespread" (3:1)? This could easily be said of our own age, as across the West faith has largely been privatized in an increasingly secular public sphere. As the last vestiges of Christendom crumble, more and more children across North America have no familiarity with the Christian Scriptures or basic Christian teachings. From generation to generation, a greater percentage of people have no connection to a religious community.[2] How will such children be reached with the good news of God's love for them and God's call to learn and walk in his ways? It will surely only happen by a renewed commitment from the church to reach children, both inside and outside the faith community, with a Christian witness of word and deed.

Parents and Grandparents as Evangelists

One of the most overlooked means of sharing the faith is the key role parents and grandparents play in the development of faith in their children and grandchildren. Samuel's parents' strong faith profoundly shaped the home into which Samuel was born and lived his first few years. Later, his parents came to pray and worship at the tabernacle where Samuel lived with Eli. They offered to Samuel an example of the faith of God's people. While the story itself doesn't delve into the influence this had on him, we know that the faith of mothers and fathers has the greatest impact on children's future religious practice.

So, how can parents and grandparents be evangelists to their children and grandchildren? Regular rhythms and practices are key: giving thanks to God before eating; reading Bible stories together; praying together as everyday worries, challenges, or thanksgivings arise; talking about our Creator when enjoying

2. Data from the Pew Research Center indicates that while self-identified Christians still outnumber religious "nones"—atheists, agnostics, or nothing in particular—by a margin of three to one in the US, as recently as 2007 this margin was five to one. Gregory A. Smith, "About Three-in-Ten U.S. Adults Are Now Religiously Unaffiliated," Pew Research Center, December 14, 2021, https://www.pewresearch.org/religion/2021/12/14/about-three-in-ten-u-s-adults-are-now-religiously-unaffiliated.

nature together; joining for worship as part of a church community; referring to Scriptures as you teach about qualities such as truthfulness, patience, kindness, goodness; and the practices of confession, forgiveness, and reconciliation. Parents can also highlight and instill Christian teachings by celebrating the seasons of the church year: Advent, Christmas, Lent, Holy Week, Easter, and Pentecost. Finally, they can demonstrate patterns of Christian study and prayer to their children as their children see them reading the Scriptures regularly, both individually and as part of a small group of Christians that meet to study and pray for each other in their home. Parents cannot ensure that their children will come to know and serve God, but they can till and enrich the soil of their children's lives, encouraging them to hear and respond to the God who calls and sends.

The Key Role of Elders as Mentors

Just as Eli mentored and guided Samuel at a critical point in his spiritual journey, adults outside a child's home can play a key role in cultivating faith in that child. Teachers can be particularly effective in this task, especially in a faith-based context. Recent data suggests that religious education, whether in religious schools, Sunday schools, or youth groups, is a factor in faith development.[3] There are many opportunities for adults to mentor and guide children and youth as they express their spiritual questions and longings and discern the voice of God calling them to know, love, and serve him.

God Speaks to and through Children

One of the most obvious lessons from the story of Samuel's conversion is that God does speak to and through children. Do we

3. A public opinion poll conducted in Canada found that 76 percent of respondents deemed "religiously committed" regularly received formal religious education outside the home, while only 43 percent of those deemed "non-believers" had done so. Korsinski, "Spectrum of Spirituality."

expect this in our highly rational and programmed approach to children today? Do churches expect that God calls children? Do we expect that children can bring us a word from the Lord? Perhaps, in light of this biblical conversion story, churches need to pray for their children to encounter God, talk with them about their own experiences of God, and give them a voice in worship services by inviting them to read the Scriptures, lead the prayers, join the choir or worship band, receive the offerings and tithes, help administer Communion, or share a word about something God has taught them recently. By meaningfully including children in the full range of worship experiences and practices not only do we cultivate these practices in their lives but we adults can hear from God through the mouths of children. Additionally, let's ask more open-ended questions in our homes that help children reflect on and express their spiritual questions, longings, and thoughts. Such questions include, "What do you think this tells us about God?" or "How do you think you would have reacted to what Jesus said?" or "Why do you think Jesus made these people angry?" or "Why do you think these first disciples followed Jesus?" In this way we parents and grandparents may also find that God has something important to say to us through the mouth of babes.

Engaging with Unchurched Families

One of the most interesting pieces of data to emerge from a recent public opinion poll in Canada indicated that of those respondents who were deemed "privately faithful"—having no connection to a faith community—64 percent of them said it was important for their children to be formally welcomed into a faith community.[4] What motivated this desire, if they themselves had no connection to such a community? Perhaps these parents wanted to give their children a choice to live as a person of faith by having a recognized organization teach them about faith. If so, how might such a family find their way into a church?

4. Korsinski, "Spectrum of Spirituality."

Churches can offer events, programs, and resources that build trust with such families. Some of these could include live nativity plays, an Easter egg hunt, an after-school homework club, a children's choir camp, sports programs, or family social events such as a movie-in-the-park night. Such families also may want to join in service and outreach projects in the neighborhood. Churches that offer a Christmas Day dinner for those who will be alone or that collect winter coats for kids in need often find that unchurched people in their neighborhood are thrilled to be invited to participate. Many parents want their children to learn about practical ways that they can help others, and churches are often already doing wonderful outreach. Churches can invite non-Christian families to participate in those projects as a way to build authentic relationships with them.

Once some trust is built with families, programming specifically focused on children and families can be offered, such as specially designed programs advertised with titles such as, "Talking to Your Kids about God" or "Meeting Superheroes of the Bible" or packaged programs such as Youth Alpha or Alpha parenting courses.[5] In recent research examining people who either committed or recommitted to Christian faith as adults, it was found that those who had been exposed to faith as children and youth were more likely to return to faith as adults.[6] This data suggests that churches can plant seeds in families and their children that may bear fruit years later. The church needs to intentionally focus on planting seeds of faith in children who are outside their immediate church community, with the hope that God will bring to life a living faith, even if this might happen years later.

Vocation as Joining in God's Mission

Finally, individual Christians, Christian families, and churches must teach children about *vocation*. God calls all of us to serve

---

5. For info on Youth Alpha, see https://alpha.org/youth. For info on Alpha parenting courses, see https://alpha.org/preview/the-parenting-children-course.
6. Stone, *Finding Faith Today*, 20.

him and our fellow human beings in all sectors of society. Whether in church leadership, education, skilled trades, health care, finance, business, manufacturing, or the arts, God is calling people to serve in every vocation so that every area of life reflects his truth and glory. Christian communities must again take seriously the task of guiding children and youth in discerning the vocation or vocations that God is calling them to. May we recall the way in which Samuel's family and Eli both helped Samuel hear God's calling on his life. The history of Israel was forever changed by his prophetic voice. May churches around the world help young people, both within and outside the church, discern what God is calling them to today.

DISCUSSION QUESTIONS

1. As a child, did you ever sense that God was in some way speaking directly to you?
2. Who are the children in your life that you might be able to share your faith with?
3. How could you make time and space for such conversations?
4. How much time each day could you spend praying for the children in your life to come to know Jesus?

8

The Conversion of a Religious Extremist

The book of Acts contains three accounts of the conversion of a man who would emerge as one of the most important leaders of the early church and one of the major writers of the New Testament: Saul, or Paul, of Tarsus.[1] To say this man's conversion was a surprise to the first Christians would be a considerable understatement. He was a zealous Pharisee who saw followers of Jesus of Nazareth as a dangerous and heretical sect within Judaism. His strong commitment to his religious faith led to his attempts to eradicate this group of people.

We first learn about Saul at a stoning in Jerusalem. He was serving as a trusted coat checker for those brutally stoning Stephen (Acts 7:58), a man chosen to lead in caring for the needy within the community of Christ followers. The record of Stephen's execution identifies Saul as an approving witness to this murder (8:1). The stoning set off widespread persecution of Christians within the

---

1. It was common in the ancient multilingual world for people to use different names depending on the context. The name Saul was a Hebrew name, while the Greek version of this name was Paul.

city of Jerusalem. Saul appears to have been at the very heart of this spate of violence and imprisonment. He is described as going house to house dragging off men and women who were disciples of Jesus (8:3). We learn of Saul's subsequent hateful actions, and his surprising turnaround, in the account of his conversion recorded in Acts 9.

Before we examine Acts 9 we should consider why there are three accounts of Paul's conversion recorded in this book. We can't know the mind of Luke, the writer of these accounts, but we can draw some conclusions based on the differences and similarities between the three narratives.[2] These differences and similarities help us explore the relationship between bearing witness to the gospel, the context in which witness occurs, and the most effective use of language.

Here "language" means more than an identifiable set of communication patterns involving sounds, vocabulary, grammatical structures, and idioms. We're interested in exploring the deeper and more complex ways in which a given language can be adapted to meet the subtle needs of communication required in different contexts.

Anyone speaking in their mother tongue makes such contextual adjustments naturally and usually without much thought. For instance, people use a different tone and cadence of voice, as well as simpler words and grammatical structures, when speaking with young children. Similarly, more formal language is used when presenting at an academic conference or in a court of law, and the language will become more colloquial and relaxed among friends over a shared meal. People adapt their language to best fit the communicative norms of the context. This sort of adaptation can be seen in the three accounts of the conversion of Paul of Tarsus.

2. I'm indebted to Marilyn Draper (Tyndale University, Toronto), who taught the evangelism course at Wycliffe College while I was on sabbatical several years ago. She suggested that a comparison of these three accounts of Paul's conversion could help students better appreciate contextualized forms of witness. I have adopted this brilliant approach and have found it to be very fruitful for students.

Let's now explore each of these three accounts of the conversion of this religious extremist, attending particularly to the intended audience and the context of that audience, to see what we can learn about evangelism. Here is the first account:

> Meanwhile Saul, still breathing threats and murder against the disciples of the Lord, went to the high priest and asked him for letters to the synagogues at Damascus, so that if he found any who belonged to the Way, men or women, he might bring them bound to Jerusalem. Now as he was going along and approaching Damascus, suddenly a light from heaven flashed around him. He fell to the ground and heard a voice saying to him, "Saul, Saul, why do you persecute me?" He asked, "Who are you, Lord?" The reply came, "I am Jesus, whom you are persecuting. But get up and enter the city, and you will be told what you are to do." The men who were traveling with him stood speechless because they heard the voice but saw no one. Saul got up from the ground, and though his eyes were open, he could see nothing; so they led him by the hand and brought him into Damascus. For three days he was without sight and neither ate nor drank.
>
> Now there was a disciple in Damascus named Ananias. The Lord said to him in a vision, "Ananias." He answered, "Here I am, Lord." The Lord said to him, "Get up and go to the street called Straight, and at the house of Judas look for a man of Tarsus named Saul. At this moment he is praying, and he has seen in a vision a man named Ananias come in and lay his hands on him so that he might regain his sight." But Ananias answered, "Lord, I have heard from many about this man, how much evil he has done to your saints in Jerusalem, and here he has authority from the chief priests to bind all who invoke your name." But the Lord said to him, "Go, for he is an instrument whom I have chosen to bring my name before gentiles and kings and before the people of Israel; I myself will show him how much he must suffer for the sake of my name." So Ananias went and entered the house. He laid his hands on Saul and said, "Brother Saul, the Lord Jesus, who appeared to you on your way here, has sent me so that you may regain your sight and be filled with the Holy Spirit." And immediately something like scales fell

from his eyes, and his sight was restored. Then he got up and was baptized, and after taking some food, he regained his strength.

For several days he was with the disciples in Damascus, and immediately he began to proclaim Jesus in the synagogues, saying, "He is the Son of God." All who heard him were amazed and said, "Is not this the man who made havoc in Jerusalem among those who invoked this name? And has he not come here for the purpose of bringing them bound before the chief priests?" Saul became increasingly more powerful and confounded the Jews who lived in Damascus by proving that Jesus was the Messiah. (Acts 9:1–22)

This first account of Saul's conversion is distinct from the other two in that it is part of Luke's broader narrative of the Acts of the Apostles. The accounts in Acts 22 and 26 record Saul himself describing his conversion to two different audiences. However, this first account in Acts 9 is Luke's telling of Saul's conversion story. So, who was Luke's audience, and how did that audience influence his choice of language?

We know from the opening verse of Acts that Luke was writing to Theophilus. "Theophilus" may well name a particular person who was a patron of Luke, someone of means, prestige, and a high rank in society who commissioned and financially supported the writing of this manuscript.[3] Biblical scholars also suggest that Theophilus, which in Greek means "lover of God," may indicate that Luke had in mind a primarily Greco-Roman audience within the early Christian community, rather than a specific person.[4] Whether written specifically for an individual patron or for the Christian community, how might the *context* of the early church have influenced how Luke shaped his account of Saul's conversion?

One of the key distinguishing features of this account, when compared to the other two accounts, is that there is no mention of Saul's religious pedigree. He is simply described as a vehement persecutor of the church who has a life-changing encounter with the risen Lord. If the primary readership of Luke's manuscript

3. Keener, *Acts*, 1:424.
4. Keener, *Acts*, 1:428.

was intended to be the church, existing as it did under the threat of persecution, it would have been encouraging to hear Jesus link himself to the persecuted church when he asked, "Saul, Saul, why do you persecute me?" (9:4). The account makes this connection a second time, as it records Paul asking, "Who are you, Lord?" The reply upended Paul's entire worldview: "I am Jesus, whom you are persecuting" (v. 5). What a powerful word of hope this would be to Christians suffering persecution. Their Lord was with them in the midst of their pain! When they were persecuted, so was he.

We read in this account several other points that would have been of interest to the young movement of Christ followers. It is peppered with signs and wonders, as well as Jewish customs that would emerge as key ecclesial practices, such as baptism and the laying on of hands in prayer. Saul was first blinded and then miraculously healed by Christ (his period of darkness mirroring Jesus's three days in the grave), when "something like scales" (9:18) fell from his eyes. Saul was then called by Christ to serve him ("he is an instrument whom I have chosen"), baptized by a disciple of Jesus (Ananias), and filled with the Holy Spirit by the laying on of hands. He was then sent by Christ to "bring my name before gentiles and kings and before the people of Israel" (9:15).

But there is even more in this story that would resonate with Luke's primary audience, the persecuted Greco-Roman church. Saul was told that he would be shown "how much he must suffer for the sake of [Jesus's] name" (9:16). Luke's audience was thus reminded that suffering is normative for followers of Christ, as demonstrated in this conversion, commissioning, and ministry of a man who once was a persecutor himself.

Luke's account concludes with Saul being "with the disciples in Damascus" (9:19), proclaiming to the Jewish community that Jesus is the Son of God and "proving that Jesus was the Messiah" (v. 22). At the forefront of this account is how his call, commissioning, and mission related to the life of the church as it struggled under persecution, began to establish its normative ecclesial practices, and discerned both its mission and who was called into leadership. This first account of Saul's conversion was perfectly shaped for a young, growing, and suffering church. Let's turn now to the other two accounts and consider a very different context, audience, and language.

"Brothers and fathers, listen to the defense that I now make before you."

When they heard him addressing them in Hebrew, they became even more quiet. Then he said:

"I am a Jew born in Tarsus in Cilicia but brought up in this city at the feet of Gamaliel, educated strictly according to our ancestral law, being zealous for God, just as all of you are today. I persecuted this Way up to the point of death by binding both men and women and putting them in prison, as the high priest and the whole council of elders can testify about me. From them I also received letters to the brothers in Damascus, and I went there in order to bind those who were there and to bring them back to Jerusalem for punishment.

"While I was on my way and approaching Damascus, about noon a great light from heaven suddenly shone about me. I fell to the ground and heard a voice saying to me, 'Saul, Saul, why are you persecuting me?' I answered, 'Who are you, Lord?' Then he said to me, 'I am Jesus of Nazareth whom you are persecuting.' Now those who were with me saw the light but did not hear the voice of the one who was speaking to me. I asked, 'What am I to do, Lord?' The Lord said to me, 'Get up and go to Damascus; there you will be told everything that has been assigned to you to do.' Since I could not see because of the brightness of that light, those who were with me took my hand and led me to Damascus.

"A certain Ananias, who was a devout man according to the law and well spoken of by all the Jews living there, came to me, and standing beside me, he said, 'Brother Saul, regain your sight!' In that very hour I regained my sight and saw him. Then he said, 'The God of our ancestors has chosen you to know his will, to see the Righteous One, and to hear his own voice, for you will be his witness to all the world of what you have seen and heard. And now why do you delay? Get up, be baptized, and have your sins washed away, calling on his name.'

"After I had returned to Jerusalem and while I was praying in the temple, I fell into a trance and saw Jesus saying to me, 'Hurry and get out of Jerusalem quickly, because they will not accept your testimony about me.' And I said, 'Lord, they themselves know that in every synagogue I imprisoned and beat those who believed in you. And while the blood of your witness Stephen was shed, I myself was standing by, approving and keeping the coats of those who killed him.' Then he said to me, 'Go, for I will send you far away to the gentiles.'" (Acts 22:1–21)

The preceding verses (21:17–40) identify the setting as Jerusalem, the audience as zealous adherents of Judaism, and the chief character as Paul, rather than Saul. But this is not to say that Paul's Jewish heritage is kept hidden in this account. Quite the opposite. Speaking in probably Aramaic,[5] the common language, Paul identifies himself as someone of fine Jewish pedigree and scholarly teaching: "I am a Jew born in Tarsus in Cilicia but brought up *in this city* at the feet of Gamaliel, educated strictly according to *our* ancestral law, being zealous for God, *just as all of you are* today" (22:3). Paul shared his personal history as someone who was raised in Jerusalem and who had studied with a leading Jewish rabbi. He mentioned his plan to take letters from the holy priest and council in Jerusalem to Jewish leaders in Damascus. These letters would have introduced Paul and given him authority to arrest disciples of Jesus (followers of "this Way") in Damascus. This authority gave him power to seize people and to bring them to Jerusalem to face trial before the religious council. Although Luke identifies him as Paul in the narrative ("then Paul said"), in Paul's own account he calls himself Saul, the Hebrew form of his name.

Another key difference between this account and the account found in Acts 9 is the description of Ananias. In this account he

5. There is scholarly debate about what language Paul was speaking here. It could well have been the Semitic language Aramaic, which was the most common language used in Jerusalem at the time and which the Hebrew people had spoken for over five hundred years. Or it could have been Hebrew, the language of the Torah, and thus known to those who studied the Torah and served in priestly roles. Craig Keener discusses this debate at length in *Acts*, 3:3191–95.

is not identified simply as a disciple, as in Acts 9, but as "a devout man according to the law and well spoken of by all the Jews living there" (22:12). Further, there is no reference to laying on of hands or infilling of the Holy Spirit; Ananias merely heals Paul using his name in Hebrew ("Brother Saul, regain your sight!," v. 13) and then pronounces his commissioning for ministry ("The God of our ancestors has chosen you to know his will, to see the Righteous One, and to hear his own voice, for you will be his witness to all the world of what you have seen and heard," vv. 14–15).

By referencing "the God of our ancestors," "the Righteous One," his return to Jerusalem, praying in the temple, and Stephen's martyrdom outside Jerusalem, Paul was highlighting the Jewish roots of the gospel and showing the crowd the bridges between them. This conversion account is given by a Jew to fellow Jews in the Holy City of Jerusalem.

We now turn to the third account of Paul's conversion cited in the book of Acts. It, too, shows evidence of being shaped for its audience:

Agrippa said to Paul, "You have permission to speak for yourself." Then Paul stretched out his hand and began to defend himself:

"I consider myself fortunate that it is before you, King Agrippa, I am to make my defense today against all the accusations of the Jews, because you are especially familiar with all the customs and controversies of the Jews; therefore I beg of you to listen to me patiently.

"All the Jews know my way of life from my youth, a life spent from the beginning among my own people and in Jerusalem. They have known for a long time, if they are willing to testify, that I have belonged to the strictest sect of our religion and lived as a Pharisee. And now I stand here on trial on account of my hope in the promise made by God to our ancestors, a promise that our twelve tribes hope to attain, as they earnestly worship day and night. It is for this hope, Your Excellency, that I am accused by Jews! Why is it thought incredible by any of you that God raises the dead?

"Indeed, I myself was convinced that I ought to do many things against the name of Jesus of Nazareth. And that is what I did in

Jerusalem; with authority received from the chief priests, I not only locked up many of the saints in prison, but I also cast my vote against them when they were being condemned to death. By punishing them often in all the synagogues I tried to force them to blaspheme, and since I was so furiously enraged at them, I pursued them even to foreign cities.

"With this in mind, I was traveling to Damascus with the authority and commission of the chief priests, when at midday along the road, Your Excellency, I saw a light from heaven, brighter than the sun, shining around me and my companions. When we had all fallen to the ground, I heard a voice saying to me in the Hebrew language, 'Saul, Saul, why are you persecuting me? It hurts you to kick against the goads.' I asked, 'Who are you, Lord?' The Lord answered, 'I am Jesus whom you are persecuting. But get up and stand on your feet, for I have appeared to you for this purpose, to appoint you to serve and testify to the things in which you have seen me and to those in which I will appear to you. I will rescue you from your people and from the gentiles—to whom I am sending you to open their eyes so that they may turn from darkness to light and from the power of Satan to God, so that they may receive forgiveness of sins and a place among those who are sanctified by faith in me.'

"After that, King Agrippa, I was not disobedient to the heavenly vision but declared first to those in Damascus, then in Jerusalem and throughout the countryside of Judea, and also to the gentiles, that they should repent and turn to God and do deeds consistent with repentance. For this reason the Jews seized me in the temple and tried to kill me. To this day I have had help from God, and so I stand here, testifying to both small and great, saying nothing but what the prophets and Moses said would take place: that the Messiah must suffer and that, by being the first to rise from the dead, he would proclaim light both to our people and to the gentiles."

While he was making this defense, Festus exclaimed, "You are out of your mind, Paul! Too much learning is driving you insane!" But Paul said, "I am not out of my mind, most excellent Festus, but I am speaking the sober truth. Indeed, the king knows about these things, and to him I speak freely, for I am certain that none of these things has escaped his notice, for this was not done in a corner. King Agrippa, do you believe the prophets? I know that you believe." Agrippa said to Paul, "Are you so quickly persuading me to become a Christian?" Paul replied, "Whether quickly or not, I pray to God that not only you but also all who are listening to me today might become such as I am—except for these chains." (Acts 26:1–29)

In this third account of Paul's conversion, we find a much different audience than in the two former accounts, and there seems also to have been a different purpose for this account. Paul is making an appeal in his own defense, while also wanting to bear witness to the good news about Jesus. His audience includes Festus, an appointed Roman proconsul or governor, King Herod Agrippa II (great-grandson of Herod the Great), Bernice (sister of Agrippa II), high-ranking military officials, and other prominent Romans. In this context, Paul is *a Jew speaking to those with great power over Jews*. It is, perhaps, the most missional of the three settings in that the key people present hold positions of influence in the broader society but are not yet followers of Jesus.

Paul directed most of his discourse toward King Herod Agrippa II, a member of the clan of Herods, who claimed Jewish heritage while also enjoying privilege and power bestowed on them by the occupying Roman Empire. Paul spoke deferentially to Agrippa, noting that he felt fortunate that it was before Agrippa that he was making his defense. Paul then referred directly to Agrippa's heritage by highlighting that Agrippa is "especially familiar with all the customs and controversies of the Jews" (26:3). Paul pointed out his own Jewish heritage and early life in Jerusalem. He noted that he belonged to "the strictest sect of our religion and lived as a Pharisee" (v. 5) and then pointed to a key belief differentiating the Pharisees from the Sadducees, "that God raises the dead" (v. 8).

Additionally, Ananias is nowhere to be found in this account. There seems to be little need to mention him to this audience. After all, which of them would care about a Jewish disciple of Jesus living in Damascus, a man of little consequence? Instead, Paul included the additional statement from Jesus, "It hurts you to kick against the goads," using the goad, a farming implement used to drive cattle, as a metaphor for the teaching, guidance, and correction of God. This well-known Greek proverb highlighted the futility of striving against either fate or a deity.[6]

While no doubt building a defense, Paul the missionary was also making a direct call for his audience (and Agrippa in particular) to "turn from darkness to light and from the power of Satan to God, so that they may receive forgiveness of sins and a place among those who are sanctified" (v. 18). Paul appealed to the "heavenly vision" he received, visions and dreams being revered as means of divine direction in the broader Greco-Roman world. But it was really to Agrippa's Jewish heritage and identity that Paul appealed, as he was "saying nothing but what the prophets and Moses said would take place: that the Messiah must suffer and that, by being the first to rise from the dead, he would proclaim light both to our people and to the gentiles" (vv. 22–23). In this account of his conversion, Paul provided an apologetic argument to people in power.

These three accounts of Paul's conversion were shaped in particular ways according to the context and audience. Each presents a distinct worldview and includes different experiences of key plot points. They also differ markedly in terms of the power held by the intended audience. What can we learn about evangelism from these three examples of witness in Scripture?

Consider Who You Are Sharing With

When Jesus shared with people about who he was, he shaped his message to them as individuals, even though the core of his message did not change. Whether talking with a socially ostracized woman at a well in Samaria or a man born blind or a Jewish religious leader who came with questions after dark, Jesus started with where they were and who they were. He did not shy away from addressing the real and pressing circumstances they were facing.

6. Keener, *Acts*, 4:3515.

In the same way, the writers of the New Testament shape their message of new life in Christ according to their intended audience. Matthew seems to have shaped his Gospel account for a predominantly Christian readership of Jewish ancestry, while Luke appears to have written for a broader readership that included both gentile and Jewish believers. Paul too seems to have been particularly skilled at translating the gospel for his conversation partner or audience. While keeping the core unchanged, he adapted his message to best relate to his particular listeners. His telling of his own conversion was shaped a little differently depending on who was listening, whether that be a crowd of Jews in Jerusalem, Greeks gathered at the Acropolis, or a small group of powerful Roman leaders. He sought to build bridges for sharing the good news about Jesus, using various people's experiences and contexts.

We too should refuse to take a one-recipe approach to sharing the gospel. We should first bathe our evangelism in prayer, asking God to make us aware of opportunities to share our faith and to show us approaches that utilize bridges that already exist between us and various listeners. Being first grounded in prayer, we must then thoughtfully consider whom we're talking to. What religious ideas and teachings, or lack thereof, have formed them as a person? What are their struggles in life? What spiritual questions and longings do they have? What have they already heard about Jesus? What has their prior experience been of Christians or the church? The answers to these questions can be helpful for knowing how best to share our own story of being changed by Jesus and his offer of salvation and transformation.

Include Your Own Story of Being Encountered by God

The gospel is one metanarrative and many micronarratives. The metanarrative is that God the Father has reconciled the world to himself through the sacrifice of Christ the Son, and the unfolding good news of that reconciliation is now empowered by the Holy Spirit. The kingdom of God—a kingdom of love, peace, joy, beauty, and fruitfulness—is already on its way. This grand metanarrative is also lived out in the particular lives of people who come to know Jesus Christ and follow him as their Lord and Savior. These micronarratives are specific to each person. They tell the story of how Christians have been encountered by God, how they came to know Jesus, and what it means to be his apprentice.

Paul began his gospel appeals to the Jews gathered in Jerusalem and to the Roman officials gathered in the halls of power with his own story of transformation on the road to Damascus. He told how he had been encountered by the risen Lord, how he had been changed, and how he was now called to live differently (micronarrative). Then he moved on to the core message concerning the good news of a Jewish Messiah who suffered, died, and was raised from the dead—a risen Lord who both calls and sends (metanarrative).

Churches ought to make space and time and encourage their members to tell each other their own gospel micronarratives. Who first told them the good news of Jesus? How did they come to believe in and follow him? How have they been changed by being a Christian and following the way of Jesus? How have they been comforted, challenged, encouraged, or corrected? What struggles have they encountered that God has helped them through? When Christians share these stories with each other, they learn how to share those stories with the many people in their lives who don't yet know Christ. Churches need to build in time for followers of Christ to share stories of faith with each other so they can grow more confident in sharing these stories with the world in need of hearing them.

Know the Story of Jesus

Churches also need to teach members about the metanarrative of the good news of Jesus, encouraging them to discuss what they find compelling about this metanarrative and giving them opportunity to tell it in their own words. What has God done for humanity through the death and resurrection of Jesus? How is the Holy Spirit at work bringing the kingdom of God into being? What makes this story so different from the claims of other belief systems?

Often churches are so busy teaching members about small sections of Scripture that they fail to ground them in the metanarrative of the Bible. We need to teach the core elements of the good news, because the world needs to hear more than just how our particular individual lives have been impacted by the gospel. They need to hear what this good news says about God's actions and intentions for the world, across all time and across every geographic, social, religious, and political division. Perhaps the simplest description of this metanarrative is that this Holy God has provided a way for us unholy human beings to draw near to him, to know him, and to love and be loved by him.

Never Stop Wanting to Tell Others about Jesus

Whether recovering from a shipwreck, trying to stay warm in a dark and dank jail cell, addressing an angry crowd, or making his defense before magistrates and rulers, Paul never stopped wanting to tell people about what God had done in Christ. The early church grew so quickly, and the gospel carried so far, because of that strong motivation for others to know and follow Jesus. And this is how the church becomes a sign, foretaste, and instrument of God's kingdom.

This same motivation drove the early Celtic missionaries to set off into stormy Irish seas. It inspired the Jesuits to carry the gospel to China and Japan. It fired up the Victorian mission societies to carry the gospel to far-flung parts of the earth. This motivation continues to drive church planters to reach the West once again with the Christian message. Imagine if every single church member across North America had a passion to share the gospel with their family, friends, colleagues, and neighbors. Imagine if we thought this was the most important message our lives could convey.

DISCUSSION QUESTIONS

1. How would you describe, in one or two sentences, the metanarrative of the gospel found in the Bible?

2. How would you describe your micronarrative, how your faith in Christ has changed you and your life?

3. How might you share Jesus contextually with (a) a close friend near death, (b) a less well-known colleague who was recently fired, or (c) a group of teens?

9

The Conversion of a Successful Businessperson

We therefore set sail from Troas and took a straight course to Samothrace, the following day to Neapolis, and from there to Philippi, which is a leading city of the district of Macedonia and a Roman colony. We remained in this city for some days. On the Sabbath day we went outside the gate by the river, where we supposed there was a place of prayer, and we sat down and spoke to the women who had gathered there. A certain woman named Lydia, a worshiper of God, was listening to us; she was from the city of Thyatira and a dealer in purple cloth. The Lord opened her heart to listen eagerly to what was said by Paul. When she and her household were baptized, she urged us, saying, "If you have judged me to be faithful to the Lord, come and stay at my home." And she prevailed upon us.

—Acts 16:11–15

What makes the Acts of the Apostles such a good read is that it zooms in on specific people, places, encounters, and conflicts. It's part travelogue, part history lesson, part character sketch. At times, it's a little like reading a diary from the first century. What the writer includes and omits in their narrative tells us something about the writer, even as it sheds light on the people and events they've written about. In this case Luke includes interactions the apostles have with both men and women, Jews and gentiles, the rich and the poor, the powerful and the powerless. Luke purposefully tells the story of missionary journeys, evangelistic witness, disciples made, and churches planted, including in his narrative what is most salient and leaving many details to be guessed at by the reader. Some stories are long, while some are very short. But these stories are not as much about the individuals as they are about the activity of God that is behind them. These stories are pieced together to form an overarching narrative of the Holy Spirit at work through the ministry of the first apostles, those sent out with a message.

The story of the conversion of the businesswoman Lydia comprises just five verses, and one of those verses is just the travelogue about how the small band of companions—Paul, Silas, Timothy, and Luke—arrived at the Roman city of Philippi. Yet even this detail is engaging, as we can imagine their journey across the Aegean Sea in an era in which itineraries and schedules were largely determined by the wind and the waves. The apostles boarded a ship sailing from Troas, stayed a night on the island of Samothrace, and set sail again for the major port of Neapolis, before heading inland, along a Roman road known as the Via Egnatia, to Philippi, in the territory of Macedonia.

Earlier in Acts 16 Luke writes that the above journey had not been the apostles' original plan. They had intended to travel northwest through the region of Asia and then head farther north. However, they were somehow "forbidden by the Holy Spirit to speak the word in Asia" (16:6). "When they had come opposite Mysia, they attempted to go into Bithynia, but the Spirit of Jesus did not allow them; so, passing by Mysia, they went down to Troas" (16:7–8).

In Troas, Paul had received a vision of a man of Macedonia urging him to come to that region. Paul and his companions understood this to be God guiding them, so they quickly adjusted their itinerary. In the vision it was a man who called them, but it was women who were the first to benefit from this change of travel plans. A woman named Lydia, whose hometown (Thyatira) was in the region of Asia the apostles had been redirected away from, was now on a collision course to meet them in the Roman colonial city of Philippi. Each one of their lives would be changed by the interaction. The Spirit was at work.

Lydia encountered Paul and his travel companions outside the city gates, at a location known to be a place of prayer. Philippi was a city in which Roman deities, including the emperor, were worshiped, and there was apparently no synagogue there.[1] Lydia, a worshiper of God, was part of a group of women gathered that day. The group likely comprised women who were either Jews or Greeks sympathetic to Judaism. They had gathered on the Sabbath near a river, a common setting for religious rituals in the ancient world. Paul and his travel companions came to this place of prayer, and they engaged this group of women in conversation.

The story gives us only select details. We are told that the men "sat down" and "spoke to the women who had gathered there" (16:13). What they said remains a tantalizing mystery. We are told the name of only one of the women, as well as her hometown (Thyatira) and her occupation (a dealer in purple cloth). We can assume she was a merchant of significant standing in the business community in Philippi. But many other details of her life remain hidden. How did she come to know about the God of Israel? What was her marital status? Why was she living in Philippi?

Biblical scholars have conjectured much about Lydia, based on their knowledge of the first-century Greco-Roman world. Craig Keener, a recognized scholar on the Acts of the Apostles, offers some key insights: Thyatira was known for dyes and its guild of dyers.[2] Lydia was likely a woman of means, since purple dye was a costly commodity made from the Murex shellfish, with a slightly cheaper version made from the red madder plant.[3] Lydia

1. Keener, *Acts*, 3:2384.
2. Keener, *Acts*, 3:2395.
3. Keener, *Acts*, 3:2399.

was likely a gentile adherent of Judaism, rather than a proselyte or convert.[4] Although as a merchant she wouldn't have been one of the true elite of Roman society in Philippi, she was a woman of some wealth, since the text indicates she owned a home large enough to host at least four guests.[5] While other facts continue to be debated, these details are relatively agreed upon by the majority of biblical scholars.

We do know that Lydia responded wholeheartedly to whatever it was that Paul told the group of women gathered by the river that day. The text tells us pointedly that "the Lord opened her heart to listen eagerly to what was said by Paul" (16:14). Then, leaping over any details about her response, any questions asked or answered, and any specifics of her conversation with Paul, we read one of the shortest transitions of any conversion story. We are simply told that "she and her household were baptized" (v. 15). That's it. And because of her speedy decision and baptism, Lydia and her household became the first converts on Paul's second missionary journey.

Exactly who this household entailed remains a mystery. But the next thing we learn is that Lydia urged Paul and his friends to come and stay at her home, which was a common way of honoring guests. Besides being a woman of some wealth, she was evidently a persuasive person, since Luke's account notes that "she prevailed upon us" (v. 15). Keener further notes that "Lydia's converted household . . . provides the foundation for the church in Philippi."[6] Despite many missing details, this story has much to teach us about how evangelization worked in the ancient world and how it can still work today.

Listen for God's Leading

We've already seen the central role played by the Holy Spirit in so many of the conversion stories of Scripture. Whether prompting

4. Keener, *Acts*, 3:2393.
5. Keener, *Acts*, 3:2404.
6. Keener, *Acts*, 3:2403.

people through dreams, visions, a godly person's guidance, or timely coincidences, God repeatedly shows himself to be the primary Evangelist. However, he invites us to participate in his mission of calling people to himself. This is why it is so important for prayer to precede any evangelistic endeavor. The church today needs to learn again the importance of discerning where God is leading. Who are the people he wants to reach through us? What bridges for the gospel might already be present in their lives? What process could best engage them and help them take steps toward knowing and serving God? Paul, Silas, Timothy, and Luke learned the importance of attending to and obeying God's direction. Lydia's story, and that of the church that would eventually meet in her home, depended on their attending to and obeying God. We must trust that God still leads today so that new people can learn of his reconciling and transforming work in their lives.

Teach Evangelistically

While we don't know what Paul said to the women gathered that day outside the gates of Philippi, we know from Paul's epistles that his teaching focused on Jesus as the Son of God, as Christ the Lord, as the one through whom Paul was called to share the faith (Rom. 1:1–5). Paul taught about being redeemed by Christ, forgiven and adopted through Christ, made alive in Christ, and empowered for service to Christ (Eph. 1). Paul preached Christ as the image of the invisible God, the firstborn over all creation, and the one through whom all things were created (Col. 1:15–16). He described Christ as the one in whom "all the fullness of God was pleased to dwell, and through him God was pleased to reconcile to himself all things, whether on earth or in heaven, by making peace through the blood of his cross" (Col. 1:19–20). Paul was clear that at the heart of the Christian faith was the Messiah, the Christ, whom the God of Israel raised from the dead and through whom he was reconciling the world to himself. At the heart of the good news is not religious rites or a list of rules but a person. When we teach people about Christianity, at the forefront should be Jesus Christ.

Accept Hospitality

In the ancient world hospitality was not only an important duty but also a key indicator of one's character. To invite someone to stay with you was more than good manners. It was a sign that you wanted to honor that person and that you yourself were a person of virtue. To have someone accept your offer of hospitality indicated they judged you to be a person of good character.[7] Lydia's offer of hospitality would have been expected for a person of financial means. She was offering her home as a base from which the ministry of Paul and his companions could proceed. We see the same sort of arrangement in Jesus's instructions to his seventy-two disciples, as he sent them out to prepare villages for his coming ministry (Luke 10:5–7). They were to receive hospitality, stay in one place, and bless that home.

It is in such interactions that deep relationships form, as people eat together, engage in casual and deep conversations, are introduced to family and friends, and have time to answer questions and model godly behavior. This slow, relational discipleship proved fruitful in the early church, and it's a great reminder that a new church starts with particular people and their network of relatives and friends. It's time again for new churches to be planted across North America. During Christendom church planting often began with a building, a pastor or priest, and an invitation to Christians of a particular denomination to become part of the new congregation. Today we need a new (and more ancient) model, in which new churches are planted around dinner tables, tables where teaching is offered, hospitality is accepted, and deep relational bonds form the foundation of new worshiping communities.

Teach and Baptize

As we have seen in the conversion of Cornelius, the Ethiopian eunuch, and now Lydia, evangelistic teaching, conversion, and

7. Keener, *Acts*, 3:2414.

baptism belong together. Baptism links new believers to the broader family of faith by a physical act that includes promises given and received. The sacrament of baptism is, first, an act of covenant between an individual and God, and second, a celebration of initiation into the church.

In some evangelical churches baptism has been sidelined and disconnected from someone becoming a follower of Jesus. In such settings baptism can easily be delayed, since the primary act of conversion is someone's "personal decision" to become a Christian. Individualism and rationalism have seeped into some churches' practices. Such thinking would have been unheard of in the early church. Even after longer catechetical teaching became the norm, when a person was deemed fit to be welcomed into the Christian faith, baptism followed. As physical beings, we have always participated in physical acts and rituals to demonstrate commitment (e.g., exchanging rings, making a vow, signing documents, wearing a distinctive item of jewelry or clothing). Across the West today, we need to reconnect evangelistic teaching, conversion, and the sacrament of baptism.

Conversion Leads to Service

While the story of Lydia's conversion spans only a few verses, this story is not the last we hear of her. After her conversion, Paul, Silas, Timothy, and Luke remained at her house while in Philippi, and her home seems to have become a base for the fledgling church in that city. In Acts 16:40 we read that when Paul and Silas were released from prison, they returned to Lydia's house, where they met with and encouraged "the brothers and sisters there" prior to their departure. Lydia's hospitality to Paul and his travel companions had been extended to other new followers of Jesus who were now gathering in her home. Her baptism into the faith was lived out in the form of servant leadership, as part of the believing community.

Many Christians in the West today view church as a gathering they go to or a service they attend so they can "be fed" and "grow spiritually." Again we see how the individualism of the broader culture has affected our view of the church of Christ. But Paul's teaching about the church uses the image of a body with many working parts, each of which plays its role for the whole body to work properly.

> The eye cannot say to the hand, "I have no need of you," nor again the head to the feet, "I have no need of you." On the contrary, the members of the body that seem to be weaker are indispensable, and those members of the body that we think less honorable we clothe with greater honor, and our less respectable members are treated with greater respect, whereas our more respectable members do not need this. But God has so arranged the body, giving the greater honor to the inferior member, that there may be no dissension within the body, but the members may have the same care for one another. If one member suffers, all suffer together with it; if one member is honored, all rejoice together with it. (1 Cor. 12:21–26)

Lydia's response to the gospel involved not only herself and her household. It also involved service to the ministry of Paul and his companions, and later to the ministry of the church in Philippi. Churches today need to again teach about the role of service to the mission of God that follows conversion. When we fail to teach and embody this connection between service, evangelism, and discipleship, we rob the church of the talents and passions of new believers. We shouldn't wait to help new believers find out how they are called to serve as part of the body of Christ.

DISCUSSION QUESTIONS

1. How would you describe Lydia to someone who had never heard her conversion story?

2. God calls both wealthy and poor people to be reconciled to him. How might this stretch people, from either of these groups, in their faith?
3. Where do you see evidence in this story of the Holy Spirit moving?
4. How have you experienced God directing your path?

10

Conversion within a Crowd

But Peter, standing with the eleven, raised his voice and addressed them, "Fellow Jews and all who live in Jerusalem, let this be known to you, and listen to what I say. Indeed, these are not drunk, as you suppose, for it is only nine o'clock in the morning. No, this is what was spoken through the prophet Joel:

> 'In the last days it will be, God declares,
> that I will pour out my Spirit upon all flesh,
>   and your sons and your daughters shall prophesy,
> and your young men shall see visions,
>   and your old men shall dream dreams.
> Even upon my slaves, both men and women,
>   in those days I will pour out my Spirit,
>   and they shall prophesy.
> And I will show portents in the heaven above
>   and signs on the earth below,
>   blood, and fire, and smoky mist.
> The sun shall be turned to darkness
>   and the moon to blood,
>   before the coming of the Lord's great and
>   glorious day.
> Then everyone who calls on the name of the Lord shall
>   be saved.'

"Fellow Israelites, listen to what I have to say: Jesus of Nazareth, a man attested to you by God with deeds of power, wonders, and signs that God did through him among you, as you yourselves know—this man, handed over to you according to the definite plan and foreknowledge of God, you crucified and killed by the hands of those outside the law. But God raised him up, having released him from the agony of death, because it was impossible for him to be held in its power. For David says concerning him,

> 'I saw the Lord always before me,
>> for he is at my right hand so that I will not be
>> shaken;
> therefore my heart was glad, and my tongue rejoiced;
>> moreover, my flesh will live in hope.
> For you will not abandon my soul to Hades
>> or let your Holy One experience corruption.
> You have made known to me the ways of life;
>> you will make me full of gladness with your
>> presence.'

"Fellow Israelites, I may say to you confidently of our ancestor David that he both died and was buried, and his tomb is with us to this day. Since he was a prophet, he knew that God had sworn with an oath to him that he would put one of his descendants on his throne. Foreseeing this, David spoke of the resurrection of the Messiah, saying,

> 'He was not abandoned to Hades,
>> nor did his flesh experience corruption.'

"This Jesus God raised up, and of that all of us are witnesses. Being therefore exalted at the right hand of God and having received from the Father the promise of the Holy Spirit, he has poured out this that you see and hear. For David did not ascend into the heavens, but he himself says,

> 'The Lord said to my Lord,
> "Sit at my right hand,
>> until I make your enemies your footstool."'

"Therefore let the entire house of Israel know with certainty that God has made him both Lord and Messiah, this Jesus whom you crucified."

Now when they heard this, they were cut to the heart and said to Peter and to the other apostles, "Brothers, what should we do?" Peter said to them, "Repent and be baptized every one of you in the name of Jesus Christ so that your sins may be forgiven, and you will receive the gift of the Holy Spirit. For the promise is for you, for your children, and for all who are far away, everyone whom the Lord our God calls to him." And he testified with many other arguments and exhorted them, saying, "Save yourselves from this corrupt generation." So those who welcomed his message were baptized, and that day about three thousand persons were added. They devoted themselves to the apostles' teaching and fellowship, to the breaking of bread and the prayers.

—Acts 2:14–42

T his Scripture passage may well be the first sermon given by one of Jesus's closest friends. Peter, an occasionally hotheaded fisherman from the village of Bethsaida on the shores of the Sea of Galilee, was once told by Jesus that he would spend the rest of his life fishing for people (Matt. 4:18–20). It seemed an unlikely prediction at the time. But this story from Acts shows just how true Jesus's words would prove to be. For on this day, on the crowded streets of Jerusalem, there would be quite a catch. What made Peter's sermon so engaging and effective? Let's delve into this fascinating story of a mass conversion to learn about the role of evangelistic preaching and how God uses sermons to draw people to himself. We begin once again with God's own activity.

The Holy Spirit Preceded Peter's Sermon

In this narrative we see yet again that God always takes the first step in the process of conversion. Luke ensures that his readers know that a mighty act of God preceded Peter's sermon. Strange signs and wonders, brought on by an outpouring of the Holy Spirit, had caused a crowd of Jews to gather. Whether residents or visitors to the city, they were present in Jerusalem to celebrate Pentecost, a great festival of pilgrimage to the temple.[1] Thousands of people attended. While the initial outpouring seems to have occurred in a second-floor room of a private home,[2] the apostles would naturally have moved to the temple courts to worship, allowing a large crowd to gather and be curious about what was happening.

They heard a group of people, all identifiable as Galileans, speaking in languages used across a wide geographic area. The passage records that the crowd was made up of Parthians, Medes, Elamites, and residents of Mesopotamia, Judea, Cappadocia, Pontus, Asia, Phrygia, Pamphylia, Egypt, Libya, and Rome. Yet they all heard these men from Galilee declaring the wonders of God in words they could understand. They were both amazed and perplexed. God, pouring out his Holy Spirit with telltale signs of wind and fire, both blessed the Christ followers and stirred up the curiosity of this diverse gathering of people.

The word chosen for "wind" in this text points to the breath of life that God alone gives.[3] Luke uses this same word later in Acts when he refers to the "life and breath that God gives" (17:25). Biblical scholars inform us that across the pagan world, wind and fire were believed to be signs of divine presence.[4] The strange proclamation in a variety of languages, by people who shouldn't have been able to do this, was further evidence of divine activity. Whatever we might say about Peter's sermon, we can say first that the amazingly fruitful sermon would never have occurred had not God first been acting. He was calling people to himself, and he wasn't afraid to use extraordinary and wondrous phenomena to do so.

1. Keener, *Acts*, 1:797.
2. Keener, *Acts*, 1:796.
3. Keener, *Acts*, 1:800.
4. Keener, *Acts*, 1:800. Here Keener points to the work of P. W. Horst, who examined a wide range of sources from the ancient world.

Peter Did Not Act Alone

It is often the curious small details in Scripture that bear rich, sometimes overlooked, fruit. The prelude to Peter's sermon notes that he was "standing *with the eleven*" (2:14). Later we read that, in response to the sermon, the people in the crowd "said to Peter *and to the other apostles*, 'Brothers, what should we do?'" (v. 37). Finally, we read that those who put their faith in Christ "devoted themselves to the *apostles'* teaching" (v. 42).

This conversion story highlights the importance of the shared vocation and leadership of those first apostles. They were gathered *together* in the upper room when the Spirit came. They experienced this wondrous movement and infilling of the Holy Spirit *together*. They stood *together* to address the crowd's questions. Their *gathered teachings* constituted the earliest catechesis and canon of New Testament Scripture for the Christian church. This passage reminds us repeatedly that Peter delivered his evangelistic sermon that day in Jerusalem as part of the ministry of a community of faith, not as the lone leader.

How Peter Got the Crowd's Attention

Once again, the small details enrich this passage. Peter, aware of the curiosity, confusion, and different interpretations being offered, addressed the crowd boldly and directly. Standing in the very heart of Judaism, with its long tradition of religious scholarship and priestly authority, this fisherman from Galilee "raised his voice and addressed them," saying, "Fellow Jews and all who live in Jerusalem, let this be known to you, and listen to what I say" (v. 14). Peter demonstrated a wonderful boldness that day. He risked himself to address the questions and assumptions of the crowd.

Having boldly grabbed their attention, Peter directly addressed the provocative accusation of drunkenness (and at nine in the morning no less!). In short, he started with where *they* were. He didn't ignore or casually dismiss their suppositions. He took them

143

seriously and then offered a different interpretation about what was happening, using cultural bridges between the apostles and the crowd.

The Cultural Bridges Peter Used

Peter began his address by referring to the ancestry and identity that he shared with the crowd, made up of both Jews gathered from the diaspora and those living in Jerusalem. They were all gathered to celebrate the festival of Pentecost. Peter appealed to these bonds throughout the sermon, addressing his audience first as "fellow Jews" (v. 14), then twice as "fellow Israelites" (vv. 22, 29), and then referencing "*our ancestor* David" (v. 29). Peter referenced David three more times in the sermon (vv. 25, 31, 34), describing the Jews' most revered king as a prophet (v. 30). Peter wanted the crowd to know that he was *with them*.

Relating Scripture to Their Present Context

After establishing the cultural bridge of a shared ancestry and identity, Peter began to connect what they were currently experiencing, as well as the recent ministry of Jesus, to Scriptures already well known to this Jewish crowd. He referenced one of their prophets (Joel 2:28–32) and then referred to the psalms (Pss. 16:8–11; 110:1). And because they were living in a time of messianic expectation, Peter offered an apologetic argument for Jesus as the promised Jewish Messiah.

In effect, Peter's sermon did what most good sermons do. He drew his listeners into Scripture to help them interpret their shared experience. He spoke of the strange and wondrous deeds of Jesus's ministry, as well as that day's strange and wondrous outpouring of the Holy Spirit. He pointed to frameworks that he shared with the crowd (e.g., the Scriptures, the prophet Joel, and King David's messianic expectations) and bridged these frameworks to a new interpretation. He wanted them to recognize Jesus of Nazareth for who he was and is: the long-promised Messiah who ministered among them, was crucified, died, and buried, but then raised from the dead to sit at God's right hand. Peter wanted them to know that this was the One who had poured out the Holy Spirit, as evidenced in the strange phenomena they were witnessing.

Peter Asked for a Response

Just as Peter's sermon began with listening to the crowd, so too the end of the sermon required further listening. But this time Peter, together with the other apostles, needed to *attend to the response* that was rippling through the crowd. They had been "cut to the heart" (v. 37) and were asking what they should do. Noticing this, Peter was very clear in his two-part direction to "repent and be baptized" (v. 38).

The word "repent" means to turn again toward God, and the religious rite associated with such repentance in the first century was baptism. Peter called for the people to respond to the message they had heard with an act of repentance. New Testament scholar Craig Keener notes, "Thus preaching repentance in Jesus' name is concretely expressed by summoning the repentant to baptism in Jesus' name, and baptism figuratively washes away sins."[5]

But how could so many people have been baptized that day? Archaeological excavations near a primary entrance to the temple mount during the time of Jesus's ministry have uncovered many *mikvaot*, ritual purification pools. These pools may have been part of a bath complex south of the temple, located near the now-blocked entrance to the temple mount. These *mikvaot* may well have been used that day for the baptisms, for there was as yet no distinction between faithful Jews and those who turned that day to Jesus as their "Lord and Messiah" (v. 36). Additionally, thirty-four ancient cisterns found near the temple mount could easily have provided the necessary water for these baptisms.[6] Finally, with Peter and the other apostles overseeing what may well have been acts of

5. Keener, *Acts*, 1:975.
6. Keener, *Acts*, 1:994.

self-immersion, such a large number of baptisms could certainly have been conducted over several hours. Here again we see a core sacrament of Christianity that has its roots in first-century Jewish practices. For many of the first Christians, evangelism, repentance, baptism, and the gifts of the Spirit were closely tied together.

Baptism as the Start of Their New Shared Life

This conversion story demonstrates that the response to Peter's sermon was much more than a heartfelt feeling of repentance followed by a religious ritual called "baptism." Baptism in Jesus's name was viewed as the beginning of a new way of life in a community made up of all the disciples of Jesus. The good news that Jesus proclaimed, of the kingdom of God breaking in on this world, became the early church's proclamation that, in Jesus Christ, God was reconciling the whole world to himself. The kingdom of God that had been long hoped for was being brought to fulfillment in and through Christ. All that was wrong was already on its way to being set right. As missiologist Lesslie Newbigin writes, the church was now being called to live "as a sign, instrument, and foretaste of God's redeeming grace for the whole life of society."[7]

This tells us much about the goal of Peter's sermon. He wanted to convey a message that would transform the way people saw both themselves and the world around them. He wanted to change the way they lived. He wanted them to know that, through the work of Christ, God now promised to forgive their sins and fill them with his Holy Spirit (v. 38). Above all, he wanted them to call upon and know the God who had done what could only be done by God, in and through Christ's birth, life, death, resurrection, and ascension.

The Importance of Evangelistic Preaching Today

This brings us to the *why* of evangelistic preaching in our own time. In his letter to the Romans, Paul highlights the importance

7. Newbigin, *Gospel in a Pluralist Society*, 233.

146

of proclamation by beginning with the goal and working backward through the means:

> But how are they *to call on* one in whom they have not believed? And how are they *to believe in* one of whom they have never heard? And how are they *to hear* without someone to proclaim him? (Rom. 10:14)

The goal, the desired end result, is for people who have not known God to *call on him*. But Paul writes that this can happen only by them coming to *believe in God*, which in turn can happen only by them *hearing* about him.

This, of course, brings us to the importance of Christians proclaiming God and his kingdom in the embodied witness of word and deed. Such proclamation refers to all manner of witness, of which evangelistic preaching is only one form. Today, as fewer people are inclined to attend church, many people are seeking answers to their spiritual questions and longings in places other than established churches. Nevertheless, there are still plenty of situations in which evangelistic sermons can be a tool used by God to call people to himself.

When Non-Christians Are Likely to Be Present

The frequent presence of explorers and seekers during a typical Sunday depends, of course, on the church. In churches with Christians who regularly talk to their friends, colleagues, and neighbors about their faith and invite them to explore it for themselves, there could well be non-Christians present every Sunday. In churches that have become overly huddled, in which no one talks with others about their faith and rarely invites someone to accompany them, weeks, months, and even years could go by without a visitor. But even in churches such as these, the Holy Spirit has a way of drawing people in from time to time.

A man out walking his dog hears a choir practicing and decides to come the next Sunday to hear the finished product. A young professional notices people chatting together as they enter a church on a Sunday morning and thinks it might be a way to meet people in her new city. An engaged couple watches a royal wedding on TV, is intrigued by God being included in the ceremony, and decides to explore church for themselves. A middle-aged man, whose wife recently died of cancer, wonders if going to church might somehow help him cope with his grief. A single mom's daughter asks a question about God that the mom doesn't know how to answer, so she takes her to church to search for a good response. Even where very few church members are sharing their faith, God, by his grace, may still draw people in. What they hear from the pulpit will greatly influence whether they return. In this sense, every sermon that gives people a glimpse of Christ and invites them to take a step toward him can be an evangelistic sermon.

There are, however, certain preaching occasions when a significant percentage, even a majority, of those in attendance will not be Christians. These occasions include funerals (especially those involving tragic deaths of the young), special memorial services such as Remembrance Day or Memorial Day (when the horror of war and the courage of self-sacrifice move us all), baptisms (when family and friends may come to show their support), weddings (when the popular vineyard spot wasn't available or when mom insisted on a "real pastor" officiating), Christmas pageants (who doesn't like to see kids dressed up as sheep and angels?), and even Christmas Eve (a time when one atheist friend told me she likes being around people who believe more than she does).

The trouble, of course, is that preachers don't always know who might show up on a Sunday morning or tune into the live stream or download a recorded sermon or attend a special service. For this reason, it's best to think of evangelistic preaching not so much as a special *type* of sermon to be preached on a special occasion (like Mission Sunday or at an evangelistic event) but as a sermon that is missionally shaped around certain hallmarks. Virtually any biblical text can be preached evangelistically when the sermon is shaped in this way.

The hallmarks of evangelistic preaching include (1) explicitly recognizing the presence of explorers, seekers, and doubters, as well as committed disciples, (2) using words and phrases that are accessible (or at least explainable) to non-Christians, (3) referring to existing cultural bridges shared with non-Christians, (4) interpreting our shared experience as human beings through the lens of Scripture, (5) focusing on the good news of God made known to us in Christ our Lord, and (6) calling people to respond to God and commit to walking in new ways. These hallmarks of evangelistic preaching are all seen in the sermon that Peter preached so effectively to the crowd gathered for Pentecost so long ago.

Acknowledge the Presence of Cynics, Seekers, and Explorers

This hallmark is relatively easy to apply to any sermon. It simply means that, while preaching, you include phrases such as "Wherever you are at with God today," "Whether you are a skeptic, an explorer, a seeker, or someone who is already a follower of Jesus," "If this is all new to you, don't worry," "Maybe it's been a long time since you thought about God," or "Maybe you're not there yet but you want to keep exploring who Jesus really is, that's fine." The key to recognizing the presence of non-Christians in an authentic way is to do so in a manner that is natural to you and that uses words and phrases that fit the context. Preachers today are most often preaching to a mixed crowd, just as Peter was on the day of Pentecost. Acknowledge that explicitly so that people know you honor them for coming just as they are.

Use Shared Cultural References

This hallmark refers to much more than including pop-culture references in a sermon, although from time to time that could be helpful. Shared cultural references are human experiences shared by the preacher and the listener. What brokenness and beauty do we see in the world around us? How do loneliness, uncertainty, broken relationships, joy, service, love, and creativity show themselves in our context? What are the primary hopes and fears that the non-Christian may have?

Peter began his sermon by listening to the crowd's questions and assumptions ("They are filled with new wine!"). He addressed that shared but erroneous assumption, helping them interpret events correctly. He used contextually appropriate cultural bridges (shared sacred texts and honored historical figures) to reveal to them what both he and they were experiencing on that extraordinary day. By doing so, he connected with them right where they were, as people curious to understand what they were seeing and hearing in the crowded temple courts and streets of Jerusalem.

Interpret Your Shared Experience through the Lens of Scripture

Another hallmark of evangelistic preaching is that it requires opening and interpreting the written Word. Preaching is not really preaching when it is simply naming the circumstances or situation of the listener and calling them to turn from that or to try harder or to deny that experience. Neither is it really preaching when it is reduced to a list of self-help tools for personal improvement or problem-solving. People can get such advice from countless sources today. Preaching requires the opening of sacred Scripture for the listener. Scripture is the foundation of every proper sermon and the lens through which preachers interpret the world. What makes a sermon evangelistic is that it attends to the assumptions of non-Christians and helps them, along with others, interpret their reality in the light of God's Word, God's ways, and God's kingdom.

Make God, Known to Us in Christ, the Primary Focus

God must be the *primary* focus of the sermon, which in turn means that most of the sermon should be focused on what the text reveals about God's nature, acts, and calling, made known to us in Jesus Christ. Skeptics, explorers, and seekers do not need therapeutic moralism. Neither do they need a list of propositions to which they must give intellectual assent. What they need is to hear about, believe in, and call upon Christ as their Lord and Savior. The task of preaching involves talking about God while also depending on God, since the conversion of the human heart is a work of God's Holy Spirit.

Give Them Some Ways to Respond to God

Realizing that you are likely to always be preaching to a mixed crowd, and trusting that the Holy Spirit has moved in such a way that some have been "cut to the heart," don't neglect to give people some concrete ways to respond to God. Such responses will depend on the context. People can respond differently during a Sunday church service than at a funeral, wedding, or other special event. There also might be denominational practices that require different forms of response. Consider carefully how listeners could respond both at the service and afterward.

For example, you might encourage them to leave their name and contact info with a church usher or at the church welcome desk or on the contact page of the church website. Or invite them to stay behind as others leave the worship gathering so you can chat with them. Perhaps you can provide information and extend a welcome for them to explore programs or upcoming events.[8] Or invite them to pray with the prayer team or to complete the newcomer card on the back of the seat in front of them. There are countless ways to help people take a next step of response as they continue their journey back to God. Above all, in the sermon itself invite them to respond to God directly through prayer. Invite them to do so with the prayer team (if you have one) or to meet you for a short prayer after the service. The goal in evangelistic preaching is for them to call on God, no matter how small the flame of belief.

8. Give them information about such things as a Blue Christmas service, a live nativity pageant, a Christmas Day dinner for those who live alone, a twelve-step program, a grief group, a parenting class, a parents and tots play group, or a singles social event.

Call Them to a New Way of Life in the Community of Faith

Finally, evangelistic preaching calls people into community, the community of people whom God is drawing to himself. Christianity is neither a spectator sport nor a solo endeavor. The new believer is initiated into the church through the water of baptism. They are baptized as followers of Jesus who commit to live in a new way, as the body of Christ. This new way involves bearing the fruit of the Spirit, such as love, joy, and peace. It involves exercising the gifts of the Spirit, such as teaching, prophecy, and works of mercy. It involves learning ancient Christian practices, such as prayer, fasting, participating in worship, sharing the Lord's Supper, studying and meditating on Scripture, and caring for the poor. Just as Peter called three thousand new believers to repentance and baptism, followed by gathering with other believers, so too evangelistic preaching needs to call people not to join a new club but to take up a new life offered to them by God as part of the body of Christ.

The above hallmarks of evangelistic preaching can be woven into almost any sermon, whether topical or exegetical. The question is, Do preachers recognize the tremendous potential to reach new people with the gospel whenever they prepare and deliver sermons? Good preaching still matters, so let's change our definition of a "good" sermon to mean one that can serve the *missio Dei* and reach those people whom God is calling to himself. Let's remember that, just as in Peter's time, effective preaching means evangelistic preaching.

DISCUSSION QUESTIONS

1. What makes a sermon memorable?
2. Do you often remember the text that was being preached?
3. Recall and briefly describe a sermon that "cut you to the heart."
4. When have you heard a preacher acknowledge that they might be preaching to a mixed crowd?

11

The Conversion of a Tormented Soul

Then they arrived at the region of the Gerasenes, which is opposite Galilee. As he stepped out on shore, a man from the city who had demons met him. For a long time he had not worn any clothes, and he did not live in a house but in the tombs. When he saw Jesus, he cried out and fell down before him, shouting, "What have you to do with me, Jesus, Son of the Most High God? I beg you, do not torment me," for Jesus had commanded the unclean spirit to come out of the man. (For many times it had seized him; he was kept under guard and bound with chains and shackles, but he would break the bonds and be driven by the demon into the wilds.) Jesus then asked him, "What is your name?" He said, "Legion," for many demons had entered him. They begged him not to order them to go back into the abyss.

Now there on the hillside a large herd of swine was feeding, and the demons begged Jesus to let them enter these. So he gave them permission. Then the demons came out of the man and entered the swine, and the herd stampeded down the steep bank into the lake and was drowned.

When the swineherds saw what had happened, they ran off and told it in the city and in the country. Then people came out to see

153

what had happened, and when they came to Jesus, they found the man from whom the demons had gone sitting at the feet of Jesus, clothed and in his right mind. And they became frightened. Those who had seen it told them how the one who had been possessed by demons had been healed. Then the whole throng of people of the surrounding region of the Gerasenes asked Jesus to leave them, for they were seized with great fear. So he got into the boat and returned. The man from whom the demons had gone out begged that he might be with him, but Jesus sent him away, saying, "Return to your home, and declare how much God has done for you." So he went away, proclaiming throughout the city how much Jesus had done for him.

—Luke 8:26–39

The story of the Gerasene demoniac is a story of juxtapositions and contrasts: Jews in a gentile territory, and a rabbi in a place of tombs and pigs. Demons who recognize Jesus and humans who don't. Madness and sanity. Mighty power and casual acquiescence. Death and life. How could such an extraordinary story of conversion have any bearing on our own ministry of evangelism today?

The answer lies in the plight of the human condition across the ages: human suffering. The need for healing and restoration ought to be a key motivation for sharing the gospel. But what exactly is the relationship between evangelism and caring for people who are suffering? In an essay exploring this question, J. Patrick Vaughn recognizes the vulnerable state of suffering people and the need to take great care so that their trust is not abused. Manipulative or mechanistic approaches to sharing the gospel could be particularly damaging in such a context. Instead, Vaughn builds a strong case for pastoral caregivers to understand themselves as evangelists. He writes, "When we ministers listen to the agonizing cries of the sick, the dying, the divorced, the depressed, the grieving, we are not simply being kind or polite. Through our care and sensitivity, we are sharing the suffering love of the triune God. We are, indeed, serving as evangelists."[1] Before we come back to this relationship between caring for suffering people and evangelism, we need to take a closer look at the person in this biblical conversion story and the profound nature of his suffering.

Human Suffering on Full Display

If there was ever someone who looked like a lost cause, it was this man. Originally from the city, he had suffered for a long time in a desolate and isolated setting, far removed from friends and family. Like a wild animal he survived naked among tombs. His maniacal violence was such that the people had restrained him with chains and shackles, but such attempts had proved fruitless against his rages. He was possessed and victimized by demons, and feared and shunned by his fellow human beings. He was a man cut off from human contact. He was cut off even from himself, for when he was asked his name, only the demons replied. This was a man who looked beyond reach.

New Testament scholar N. T. Wright offers a particularly graphic translation of the man's initial interaction with Jesus: "'You and me, Jesus. You and me!' he yelled at the top of his voice. 'What is it with you and me, you son of the Most High God? Don't torture me—please, please don't torment me!'"[2] This desperate plea came out of the man when Jesus commanded the unclean spirit to come out of him (Luke 8:29). Then Jesus said something to the man that he likely hadn't heard for a long time: he asked him his name. The chilling response was simply "Legion."

A Roman legion was a regiment of six thousand soldiers, a terrifying display of power. Yet Jesus was unfazed by the response of this Legion. After all, he had intentionally come to this place of death, demons, and swine, a place of defilement for any respectable Jewish rabbi. Yet it was in this place that Jesus again demonstrated his power to command demons and to direct their

1. Vaughn, "Evangelism," 271.
2. Wright, *Luke for Everyone*, 99.

movement. Acquiescing to their request to enter a nearby herd of pigs, Jesus commanded it to be so. Yet even within the pigs, death and destruction was the demonic result, as they plunged into the Sea of Galilee and drowned. No wonder the pig farmers rushed to tell others about these strange events. And no wonder a crowd came out to see for themselves what had occurred.

Human Fear on Full Display

What they saw next terrified them. This violent, maniacal man, known and feared for many years, was now clothed and sitting at the feet of this new arrival, Jesus of Nazareth. From across the Sea of Galilee, a person with power greater than the Gerasene demoniac had come to their region. Perhaps it was the strange power of this rabbi that scared the townspeople. Perhaps the tombs, long viewed as a place of spirits, contributed to that fear. Perhaps the pig farmers were afraid that this Jewish teacher was deliberately targeting them and their livelihood. What other economic costs might they as a community incur because of this stranger's presence in their midst?

We can't know what the Gerasene people were thinking. All we know is that they asked Jesus to leave, and he complied. However, there was one person Jesus instructed to remain in that community: the man who had been healed and restored to his right mind. The last words Jesus spoke to him were his commissioning to be a witness to his own people, telling them everything *God* had done for him. The text then draws a direct link between God the Father and God the Son when it reveals that the man "went away, proclaiming throughout the city how much *Jesus* had done for him" (8:39). This man, alienated from his community and enslaved to forces beyond himself, was now clothed and returning to his hometown. He had become a disciple, learning at Jesus's feet. He had been restored in body, mind, and soul. Now he had been sent out to witness to others. Let's now explore key lessons about evangelism that can be found in this remarkable story of conversion and how they can impact witness in our own time.

Evil Seeks to Destroy Both Individuals and Communities

This story of conversion unsettles our modern sensibilities because it unveils a supernatural realm and reality beyond our knowledge and control. As scientifically minded moderns, we have rational and natural explanations for everything. So, what do we make of the Bible's many accounts of demons and angels, visions and dreams, that point to a realm beyond our natural world? Can all biblical stories involving demons be explained away as forms of mental illness (e.g., schizophrenia) or some other physical malady (e.g., epilepsy)? Can visions and dreams be simply reduced to hallucinations, wishful thinking, or the brain working through its anxieties?

While biblical stories of demon possession hint that at least some of the experiences described are linked to psychological or physical illness, many of these stories simply give too little detail to determine what resulted in the person's experience. We want to be able to safely dispel the notion that there are spiritual forces beyond our control, but the Scriptures suggest that these forces do exist. There are forces at work in the world that seek to harm individuals, communities, humanity, even the whole of creation. Additionally, the Scriptures point to God as the only being who can powerfully defeat such negative spiritual forces.

The Anglican liturgy of baptism requires candidates to renounce three things: (1) "Satan and all the spiritual forces of wickedness that rebel against God," (2) "the evil powers of this world which corrupt and destroy the creatures of God," and (3) "all sinful desires that draw you from the love of God."[3] These three *renunciations*, each one more personal than the one before it, are followed by three *affirmations* of Jesus as their gracious and loving Savior and Lord. The point of these renunciations and affirmations is the ancient idea that turning toward God requires us to acknowledge and renounce evil, both around us and within us. These words explicitly state something that the Bible also clearly expresses. Evil is real, and whether it comes in the form of individual or societal torment, it brings about devastating effects.

3. Anglican Church of Canada, *Book of Alternative Services*, 154.

The story of the Gerasene demoniac gives us no clue as to the cause of this man's possession by demons. Whether linked to childhood or adult trauma, mental illness, or some other foothold, his demons were real, and they were causing great suffering. Fear permeates the story. The man is afraid that Jesus will torment him. The demons are fearful of being forced back into the abyss. The pig farmers are fearful for their livelihood. And the townspeople are fearful of a healing power they cannot understand. The only one who was not fearful was Jesus. He calmly healed and restored the tormented man.

The question for the church to ask itself is, Do we believe that evil is indeed real, and do we believe that God has the power to heal people from its effects? If we do, this will empower our proclamation of the good news of Jesus Christ, in both our words and deeds. The way God chooses to heal may vary, but the proclamation and celebration of God's power to heal, and the church's calling to be a sign, foretaste, and instrument of that restoration, is at the core of the gospel message. It's a message to be proclaimed even to those who look like they are beyond reach.

Jesus Is *For* Those Who Look like Lost Causes

At its best, the church across the ages has ministered to people whom society regarded as beyond help. Abandoned newborns were adopted and nurtured, people with leprosy were given food and lodging, and victims of plagues were provided with palliative care or a proper burial. From medieval monks in monasteries to Mother Teresa's nuns on the streets of Calcutta, the rejects of society have found the love of God expressed through the hospitality and loving care of Christians. The church has done this because this is what we saw the Lord doing and this is what the Lord commanded. The Good Shepherd went out looking for the one lost sheep to bring it home, and he didn't seem to care if others thought it was beyond reach.

Jesus touched a man with leprosy and commanded life to return to a dead child. He made a mute boy speak and caused a paralyzed man to walk again. He opened the eyes of someone born blind and caused a dishonest tax collector to turn over a new leaf. Each person had likely been written off as beyond hope by almost everyone. But these were the sorts of people Jesus seemed to especially seek out. The story of the demoniac's conversion ought to remind us of this fact. The church is not supposed to be a club for the like-minded and similarly dressed. The church is to be a refuge for the weary, a hospice for the dying, a hospital for the sick, a school for the curious, a temple for the worshiper, and a family for the orphan.

Why Jesus Comes to Us

The question that the man in this story screamed at Jesus is deeply significant for us today: "What have you to do with me, Jesus, Son of the Most High God?" (8:28). As the last vestiges of power and privilege bestowed on the church during Christendom disappear, especially in North America, a religiously pluralistic yet publicly secular society will need to grapple with this question. Can we continue to instill values that grew out of a Judeo-Christian world-view if we abandon that worldview for one based on secularism, individualism, and consumerism? How will such a society view its most needy members if the person and teachings of Jesus, who demonstrated (and commanded) love for such people, are thought to be irrelevant now? Can we have his values without having *him*? And perhaps more importantly, can the church continue to remember how to be disciples of Jesus in such a society?

In this story of conversion, a person returns to his "right mind" because he is encountered by Jesus. From a naked, fearful, and alienated man beset by demons and taking shelter in a graveyard, he was transformed into a man clothed and at peace. Returning to his home, he was determined to live as a witness to the transform-ing power of Jesus. In Jesus, he had found his true identity as a human being. This story teaches us that it is out of love that Jesus comes to people, just as he came to this man. His love is such that he seems to especially care about the most deranged, despised, feared, and even violent human beings. There is no one who is a "lost cause" to Christ. All can discover who they were created to be. Such is one of the sweet fruits of discipleship: people discover themselves renewed.

Jesus referred to this renewal as a spiritual new birth,[4] and it is his desire that the whole world should experience this reconciliation and healing. Has the church in the West forgotten that the goal of discipleship is not full pews but transformed lives? In Jesus there is a power like no other. The early church, and Christians down through the centuries, have understood Jesus to be God incarnate, born among us. The Gospels and the book of Acts record the extraordinary power that people experienced in and through Christ. But we also know from this story that not everyone viewed Jesus in this way. There were people that day who rejected Jesus.

The Possibility of Rejecting Jesus

It is important to reckon with the possibility that people will reject Jesus as we seek to share the gospel in our own time. The swineherds were more concerned about their herd of pigs than they were about the transformative power they had witnessed in a fellow human being. The people who rushed to see for themselves what had happened were so afraid that they asked Jesus to leave. People may well reject the good news, even when they have evidence of its power right before them. But I wonder about the people who rejected Jesus that day. Left in their midst was a powerful witness to the transforming power of God. When people reject Jesus today, we should always remember that they may well come to him tomorrow.

The Powerful Witness of a Changed Life

Jesus complied with the request to leave the region of the Gerasenes that day. But he cared enough about the swineherds, the

---

4. See Jesus's conversation with the religious leader Nicodemus in John 3.

townspeople, and others in that region that he left a witness. Down through the ages there have been key witnesses, and over time the Spirit has been at work in such people. The powerful witness of a life transformed is hard to deny. No well-constructed argument was ever more convincing than a living, breathing example of God's healing and reconciling power. As we look across the conversion stories of Scripture, we see countless people who were forever grateful that they had been encountered by and transformed by Jesus. Many of these stories mention their subsequent witness to fellow villagers, friends, and family members. Their gratitude compelled them to share with others the good news of their healing and transformation. It remains true today that the most effective evangelism often results from the overflow of a grateful heart. Perhaps the renewal of the church's witness will rest on Christians across the West answering for themselves, and then for their non-Christian neighbors and friends, "How has my encounter with Jesus Christ transformed me?"

DISCUSSION QUESTIONS

1. If you had been traveling with Jesus across the Sea of Galilee that day, how do you think you would have responded to the man from the tombs?
2. In what way have you been changed by Jesus?
3. What ministries to hurting people (e.g., grief support groups, divorce-care programs, addiction support groups, counseling and therapy funding, a regular service of prayer for healing) are offered by your church?

12

The Great Commission Revisited

Now the eleven disciples went to Galilee, to the mountain to which Jesus had directed them. When they saw him, they worshiped him, but they doubted. And Jesus came and said to them, "All authority in heaven and on earth has been given to me. Go therefore and make disciples of all nations, baptizing them in the name of the Father and of the Son and of the Holy Spirit and teaching them to obey everything that I have commanded you. And remember, I am with you always, to the end of the age."

—Matthew 28:16-20

For at least two centuries the text we now call the Great Commission has been cited as the *raison d'être* of evangelism and mission. But this text was not always viewed this way. As missiologist David Bosch has pointed out, for long stretches of church history, this text was interpreted as a commission given specifically to the first apostles and was considered binding only on them. Even more astonishingly, this Scripture passage was even viewed as *fulfilled* by them, since the apostles had taken the gospel throughout the ancient world during their time. Bosch notes that, by arguing that the office of apostle ended with the death of those first apostles, Luther and Calvin helped to further solidify the view that this text was limited in its scope.[1] Amazingly, "when Justinian von Welz in 1664 published a plea in which he advocated, on the basis of Matthew 28:16–20, for a worldwide missionary enterprise, his views were dismissed by Johann H. Ursinus as advocating interference with God's plan for the nations."[2]

William Carey turned this view of Matthew 28:16–20 on its head when in 1792 he published *An Enquiry into the Obligations of Christians to Use Means for the Conversion of the Heathens.* Bosch credits Carey's argument as key to launching the large-scale Protestant missionary endeavor from Europe and North America that reached around the world.[3] The Great Commission became a foundational text, cited by Roman Catholic, Anglican, and Protestant missionary societies everywhere.

Bosch notes that the motivational impetus applied to this text by Carey and others was one of *obedience* to a divine command. Bosch points to key words and phrases used in Carey's *Enquiry* that were repeated throughout missionary literature and were still evident in the address of the evangelical Anglican scholar John Stott at the World Congress on Evangelism in Berlin in 1966:

> In the last resort, we engage in evangelism today not because we want to or because we choose to or because we like to, but because we have been told to. The Church is under orders. The risen Lord has commanded us to "go" to "preach," to "make disciples," and that is enough for us.[4]

But is obedience to a command the only, or even the preferred, lens through which to view the Great Commission? Bosch, citing such missional leaders as Roland Allen and Lesslie Newbigin, builds an argument for interpreting this text less through the lens of an *obligation* and more through the lens of a *promise* arising

1. Bosch, "Structure of Mission," 73.
2. Bosch, "Structure of Mission," 74.
3. Bosch, "Structure of Mission," 74.
4. Stott, "Great Commission," 37.

from the authority of Christ and his promised presence in his church.[5] This interpretation seems to mesh with Acts 1:8, which uses the language of promise, rather than command: "But you will receive power when the Holy Spirit has come upon you, and *you will be my witnesses* in Jerusalem, in all Judea and Samaria, and to the ends of the earth."

Bosch argues for a deeply contextualized and incarnational model grounded in the presence of God with his church, as well as the servanthood of disciples who are themselves being discipled. Bosch contends that a careful exegesis of Matthew 28:16–20 suggests a framework in which

> mission (or disciple-making) avoids becoming a heavy burden, a new law, a command to obey. The disciples' involvement in mission is a logical consequence of their being "discipled unto Jesus" and of the "full authority" given to him (notice the "therefore" in Matt. 28:19). "You are my witnesses because you have been with me" (John 15:27). To be involved in mission is to receive a gift, not to obey a law; to accept a promise, not to bow to a command.[6]

But is such a model of mission, in which disciple-making is seen as a *promise* grounded in God's own work of drawing people to himself, apparent in the biblical stories of conversion? As we have already seen, the conversions of Cornelius, the Ethiopian eunuch, Paul of Tarsus, Lydia, the Gerasene demoniac, and the thousands drawn to Christ at the feast of Pentecost certainly support this model. What we see over and over again in Scripture is that God is the primary Evangelist, and the church joins in God's work out of joyful *gratitude* for their own transformation. We now turn to yet another biblical story of conversion to further explore this framework for interpreting the Great Commission.

> Now when Jesus learned that the Pharisees had heard, "Jesus is making and baptizing more disciples than John" (although it was

---

5. Bosch, "Structure of Mission," 76.
6. Bosch, "Structure of Mission," 91.

not Jesus himself but his disciples who baptized), he left Judea and started back to Galilee. But he had to go through Samaria. So he came to a Samaritan city called Sychar, near the plot of ground that Jacob had given to his son Joseph. Jacob's well was there, and Jesus, tired out by his journey, was sitting by the well. It was about noon.

A Samaritan woman came to draw water, and Jesus said to her, "Give me a drink." (His disciples had gone to the city to buy food.) The Samaritan woman said to him, "How is it that you, a Jew, ask a drink of me, a woman of Samaria?" (Jews do not share things in common with Samaritans.) Jesus answered her, "If you knew the gift of God and who it is that is saying to you, 'Give me a drink,' you would have asked him, and he would have given you living water." The woman said to him, "Sir, you have no bucket, and the well is deep. Where do you get that living water? Are you greater than our ancestor Jacob, who gave us the well and with his sons and his flocks drank from it?" Jesus said to her, "Everyone who drinks of this water will be thirsty again, but those who drink of the water that I will give them will never be thirsty. The water that I will give will become in them a spring of water gushing up to eternal life." The woman said to him, "Sir, give me this water, so that I may never be thirsty or have to keep coming here to draw water."

Jesus said to her, "Go, call your husband, and come back." The woman answered him, "I have no husband." Jesus said to her, "You are right in saying, 'I have no husband,' for you have had five husbands, and the one you have now is not your husband. What you have said is true!" The woman said to him, "Sir, I see that you are a prophet. Our ancestors worshiped on this mountain, but you say that the place where people must worship is in Jerusalem." Jesus said to her, "Woman, believe me, the hour is coming when you will worship the Father neither on this mountain nor in Jerusalem. You worship what you do not know; we worship what we know, for salvation is from the Jews. But the hour is coming and is now here when the true worshipers will worship the Father in spirit and truth, for the Father seeks such as these to worship him. God is spirit, and those who worship him must worship in spirit and truth." The woman said to him, "I know that Messiah is coming" (who is called Christ). "When he comes, he will proclaim all things to us." Jesus said to her, "I am he, the one who is speaking to you."

Just then his disciples came. They were astonished that he was speaking with a woman, but no one said, "What do you want?" or, "Why are you speaking with her?" Then the woman left her water jar and went back to the city. She said to the people, "Come and see a man who told me everything I have ever done! He cannot be the Messiah, can he?" They left the city and were on their way to him.

Meanwhile the disciples were urging him, "Rabbi, eat something." But he said to them, "I have food to eat that you do not know about." So the disciples said to one another, "Surely no one has brought him something to eat?" Jesus said to them, "My food is to do the will of him who sent me and to complete his work. Do you not say, 'Four months more, then comes the harvest'? But I tell you, look around you, and see how the fields are ripe for harvesting. The reaper is already receiving wages and is gathering fruit for eternal life, so that sower and reaper may rejoice together. For here the saying holds true, 'One sows and another reaps.' I sent you to reap that for which you did not labor. Others have labored, and you have entered into their labor."

Many Samaritans from that city believed in him because of the woman's testimony, "He told me everything I have ever done." So when the Samaritans came to him, they asked him to stay with them, and he stayed there two days. And many more believed because of his word. They said to the woman, "It is no longer because of what you said that we believe, for we have heard for ourselves, and we know that this is truly the Savior of the world." (John 4:1–42)

This story of the amazing conversion of one woman and many people in her community shows us Jesus's own model of evangelism. The encounter was also a teaching moment for Jesus's disciples, and it was significant enough that it was included in John's Gospel. What are the hallmarks of Jesus's approach to evangelism that can be seen in this story?

Jesus Engaged

The meeting between Jesus and the Samaritan woman seems to have been more than happenstance, as the text notes in detail the particular circumstances that resulted in this unusual encounter. Jesus was returning to Galilee due to opposition and threats from the Pharisees in Judea. Although the reason is not indicated, it was necessary for Jesus to travel through Samaria. Traveling the well-worn route, Jesus's group stopped in the heat of the day at Jacob's well, in the Samaritan city of Sychar. Jesus was tired, thirsty, and alone, since his disciples had gone into Sychar to purchase food. Although it was an unusual time to collect and carry water, a woman had come to the well at noon. The text doesn't explicitly say that Jesus had deliberately sought this woman out, but the odd timing and setting, together with Jesus's direct engagement with her, seems to echo several other encounters in which surprising people are sought out and engaged by Jesus.

Jesus Crossed Cultural Boundaries

Like Jesus's encounter with the Gerasene demoniac, this encounter broke several cultural rules of engagement. Just as Jewish rabbis would normally have avoided a place of tombs and pigs, they normally would have avoided talking to Samaritans, especially a solitary Samaritan woman. The disciples' surprise when they returned from buying food and found Jesus talking with such a woman further highlights the cultural taboos being ignored. Yet Jesus was not concerned about crossing the cultural boundaries of religion or gender. The person before him was what mattered.

Jesus's Contextualized and Deeply Christocentric Approach

There are several things about this conversation that reveal Jesus's ability to connect deeply with people in their own context. He met the woman at the well from which she drew water, even though it was burdensome for her to do so. The gathering of water from such wells was essential work in her culture, and it was predominantly women's work. But whereas most women gathered water in the cooler parts of the day, she had come at noon, when the fewest number of people would be present. We can't be sure why she had come at that specific time, but commentators have suggested that, as a woman who had been married five times and was now living with someone who was not her husband, she was likely socially marginalized and may have wanted to avoid social contact. Jesus alone was present to meet her in her complicated and shameful context.

He asked a favor of her, opening himself up to hospitality or rejection. He engaged with her about her painful personal life, asking her to go and get her husband. He also engaged with her on matters of faith. Jesus didn't whitewash the differences between Samaritans and Jews, but he used a key theological bridge between them to point the conversation toward himself: belief in the coming Messiah. It was to this woman that Jesus made one of the clearest statements about his identity, "I am he, the one who is speaking to you" (4:26). This statement clarified his earlier comments: "If you knew the gift of God and who it is that is saying to you, 'Give me a drink,' you would have asked him, and he would have given you living water" (v. 10) and "Those who drink of the water that I will give them will never be thirsty. The water that I will give will become in them a spring of water gushing up to eternal life" (vv. 12–13). Having started the conversation by recognizing her particular context, he nevertheless focused primarily on his identity as the Christ, the long-awaited Anointed One.

The Woman's Response

The Samaritan woman's attitude changed from cynicism and suspicion to wonderment, joy, and witness for Jesus. There is no hint of witness being a duty or obligation. This woman, who seemed to previously be avoiding personal contact, now rushed to tell everyone. She was in such a hurry to do so that she left behind her jar. Nowhere in the text did Jesus command her to go and tell her community. She bore witness to Jesus in response to having been encountered by him, seen by him, and changed by him. Here we see evangelism overflowing from a grateful heart.

Her Community's Response

The reaction of her fellow villagers is also instructive. After the woman's witness sparked their curiosity, they came to explore for themselves and asked Jesus to stay longer. After spending two days with him, they bore their own witness to the one they now knew was "the Savior of the world." The progression of their belief in Jesus echoes the same progression in the story of the man who had been blind since birth (John 9). At first Jesus was viewed as a Jewish man, then as a prophet, and finally as the Savior of the world. Whenever people came to understand who Jesus was, they seemed to take joy in telling others about him. Being encountered and transformed by Jesus inspired the witness in this and many other conversion stories. Could this fact hold the key to understanding the Western church's complacency about evangelism and mission in our own time?

Duty Is a Poor Substitute for Love

It would be erroneous to argue that there is no command present in the Great Commission. The text's plain reading is, "Go therefore and make disciples of all nations" (Matt. 28:19). This link between being a Christian and being ready to witness for Christ is echoed in other New Testament Scriptures. In 1 Peter 3:15 we read, "But in your hearts sanctify Christ as Lord. Always be ready to make your defense to anyone who demands from you an accounting for the hope that is in you." This verse assumes that a witness of hopefulness is supported by a readiness to offer a respectful apologetic for the faith. But even this command to offer a cogent and respectful defense is assumed to follow an observable difference in one's behavior. Christians are to be people of observable hope.

In 1 Corinthians 9:16 we read Paul's own sense of duty to bear witness for Christ: "If I proclaim the gospel, this gives me no ground for boasting, for an obligation is laid on me, and woe to me if I do not proclaim the gospel!" One could argue that Paul had a specific commissioning (like the other apostles) to bear witness for Christ, and so this verse has limited application to all Christians. But just who today will come to faith if Christians do not proclaim the gospel? The church in the West cannot deny that its general avoidance of evangelism is directly correlated to its decline. Wouldn't it be wise for the church to again preach that all Christians have a *duty* to share the faith?

Perhaps an analogy would help us understand the role of duty in evangelism. Duty has a place in a marriage. For instance, having a sense of duty to honor one's wedding vows can help us work through differences and persevere through challenges, even when we don't feel like it. But duty is a poor motivator over the long haul. Which of us would boast of a husband or wife who is staying with us purely out of duty? Duty is a poor substitute for love.

The same is true for evangelism. As with the Samaritan woman at the well, a love for Christ, resulting from our encountering of him, must be our impetus for sharing the good news of Jesus. God is reconciling the world to himself, and we are invited to join in that work by serving as Christ's ambassadors, through whom God is making his appeal to others. "So we are ambassadors for Christ, since God is making his appeal through us; we entreat you on behalf of Christ: be reconciled to God" (2 Cor. 5:20). This verse points to God as the Evangelist. He is making *his appeal* to others to be reconciled to him and to serve him in their lives. We are simply his representatives, sent out with a message of good news about the Anointed One, the Messiah, to share with the world.

God's Authority, Activity, and Presence as the Primary Catalyst

The Great Commission begins and ends with Jesus. Yes, we have a part to play, joining in God's great work by making disciples, baptizing, and teaching. But our witness ultimately is grounded in Jesus as the One to whom "all authority in heaven and on earth has been given" and who promises to be with us "always, to the end of the age." The more we focus on Jesus, the clearer and more compelling our message will be to the outside world.

But how can the church be brought to a deeper place with God so that this can happen?

Our Calling Is to Attend to God with Wonderment, Joy, and Gratitude

The church in the West needs to be more deeply grounded in the Scriptures (as the story of God), in prayer (listening to and speaking with God), and in worship (offering our lives daily to God). We need to raise the bar of biblical literacy, the practice of daily prayer, and worship that is offered in spirit and in truth. When the church in the West comes alive to the reality of Christ, as the Samaritan woman did on that day so long ago, our surrounding communities will come alive with curiosity and begin to experience and know Jesus for themselves.

DISCUSSION QUESTIONS

1. Describe when you first came to know Jesus.
2. What was it about Jesus that you found most compelling?
3. Why do you think Jesus said to the disciples: "But I tell you, look around you, and see how the fields are ripe for harvesting. The reaper is already receiving wages and is gathering fruit for eternal life, so that sower and reaper may rejoice together. For here the saying holds true, 'One sows and another reaps.' I sent you to reap that for which you did not labor. Others have labored, and you have entered into their labor" (John 4:35–38)?
4. What thoughts and/or feelings does the following statement stir up in you: "In Christ God was reconciling the world to himself" (2 Cor. 5:19)?

13

How and Why Jesus Sends Us Out as His Church

The church in the West faces many challenges: declining church attendance, surplus and deteriorating church buildings, and a rise in competing spiritualities. Further, there is widespread suspicion about institutions in general, whether political, legal, medical, educational, or religious, and that affects the church too. Although globally millions have been lifted from poverty through improved agriculture, health care, and education, there is a sense of societal decline as wealth inequality continues to increase. Finally, the world continues to struggle with global supply chain challenges, labor shortages, political and military conflicts, climate crises, and increasing societal polarization. The global pandemic exacerbated many of these forces.

How will the church reimagine itself as the last traces of Christendom fade and Christianity becomes simply one religious or spiritual option among many? How will the church's missional practices of evangelism need to change for it to fulfill its apostolic calling? While the Scriptures assure us that God continues the work of reconciling the world to himself and that one day this work will be complete, the path toward that day is shrouded in mystery. Perhaps looking back to an ancient though similar setting will help us chart the way forward. The Scripture passage we will explore in this final chapter was written during a time when religious pluralism was the norm, when political unrest and crushing economic inequality abounded, and when the church was struggling to find a foothold.

In this context Jesus sent out seventy-two of his disciples to share the good news of the kingdom of God in the villages and towns of first-century Galilee. What can we learn about whom he selected and sent, how they were to approach people, and the message they were to convey? What cautions did Jesus give them about engaging in this great endeavor? Let's explore this extraordinary passage from Luke's Gospel with the hope of learning how we can again reach people for Christ in our own time.

After this the Lord appointed seventy-two others and sent them on ahead of him in pairs to every town and place where he himself intended to go. He said to them, "The harvest is plentiful, but the laborers are few; therefore ask the Lord of the harvest to send out laborers into his harvest. Go on your way; I am sending you out like lambs into the midst of wolves. Carry no purse, no bag, no sandals, and greet no one on the road. Whatever house you enter, first say, 'Peace to this house!' And if a person of peace is there, your peace will rest on that person, but if not, it will return to you. Remain in the same house, eating and drinking whatever they provide, for the laborer deserves to be paid. Do not move about from house to house. Whenever you enter a town and its people welcome you, eat what is set before you; cure the sick who are there, and say to them, 'The kingdom of God has come near to you.' But whenever you enter a town and they do not welcome you, go out into its streets and say, 'Even the dust of your town that clings to our feet, we wipe off in protest against you. Yet know this: the kingdom of God has come near.' I tell you, on that day it will be more tolerable for Sodom than for that town.

"Woe to you, Chorazin! Woe to you, Bethsaida! For if the deeds of power done in you had been done in Tyre and Sidon, they would have repented long ago, sitting in sackcloth and ashes. Indeed, at the judgment it will be more tolerable for Tyre and Sidon than for you. And you, Capernaum,

> will you be exalted to heaven?
> No, you will be brought down to Hades.

"Whoever listens to you listens to me, and whoever rejects you rejects me, and whoever rejects me rejects the one who sent me."

The seventy-two returned with joy, saying, "Lord, in your name even the demons submit to us!" He said to them, "I watched Satan fall from heaven like a flash of lightning. Indeed, I have given you authority to tread on snakes and scorpions and over all the power of the enemy, and nothing will hurt you. Nevertheless, do not rejoice at this, that the spirits submit to you, but rejoice that your names are written in heaven."

At that very hour Jesus rejoiced in the Holy Spirit and said, "I thank you, Father, Lord of heaven and earth, because you have hidden these things from the wise and the intelligent and have revealed them to infants; yes, Father, for such was your gracious will. All things have been handed over to me by my Father, and no one knows who the Son is except the Father or who the Father is except the Son and anyone to whom the Son chooses to reveal him."

Then turning to the disciples, Jesus said to them privately, "Blessed are the eyes that see what you see! For I tell you that many prophets and kings desired to see what you see but did not see it and to hear what you hear but did not hear it." (Luke 10:1–24)

Jesus had previously sent out the original twelve disciples to preach and heal (Luke 9:1–6; Mark 6:7–12). Now, the Gospel of Luke records Jesus sending out seventy-two disciples to do the same.[1] Why would Jesus send out this specific number? Biblical scholars have suggested that this number was loaded with symbolic meaning, since this was thought to be the number of nations that existed when Luke's Gospel was written.[2] If so, that number

1. Some translations record this number as seventy, reflecting variations among the oldest available manuscripts.
2. Marshall, *Gospel of Luke*, 413.

would have been a reminder that the good news of the kingdom of God is for everyone. Perhaps the church throughout the West needs to be reminded of this truth. While this passage has inspired missionaries to carry the gospel to nations all over the globe, it should equally compel us to consider the people in our own neighborhoods, workplaces, and social networks who have yet to know Jesus as Savior and Lord.

Jesus sent these seventy-two disciples to the villages and towns that he himself intended to visit, although the text doesn't say when and how this was to happen. Were these seasoned disciples, or were they relatively new to following Jesus? The text doesn't reveal anything about his selection process, which suggests that Jesus may not have been all that particular. Those who were called to be disciples were called to prepare the way for him. He sent them in pairs perhaps for mutual support and encouragement, because he knew the task was not easy. However, some scholars suggest that it may have been because Judaism required two witnesses to testify to events, which would have given greater credibility to the various reports they gave upon their return.[3]

Was Jesus's description of them being sent out as "lambs into the midst of wolves" (10:3) a warning of mortal danger (emphasis on the wolves)? Or was it an instruction to make themselves particularly vulnerable (emphasis on the lambs)? While opposition was certainly a possibility, the other instructions Jesus gave the seventy-two disciples seem to suggest a call to vulnerability. They were to take no extra money, clothing, or shoes. They were to trust both in God's provision and in the hospitality of the people in the towns and villages they were visiting. They were to focus on their task of reaching and providing witness to their assigned communities, and they were not to be distracted by fellow travelers on the road. When offered lodging, they were to stay in that house and accept with gratitude whatever food they were given.

The message they bore was good news. It included a blessing of peace on the household that received them and a proclamation

3. Marshall, *Gospel of Luke*, 416.

to the community that the kingdom of God had come near. They were also to heal the sick, a tangible demonstration of their presence and proclamation being grounded in the power of God. If they were in fact rejected, they were to offer a warning by wiping the dust from their feet. But this was to be paired with a proclamation to their rejectors that the kingdom of God had come near.

Upon returning, the disciples' reports to Jesus were a source of great joy, and he "rejoiced in the Holy Spirit" (10:21). (I wonder what it looked like to see Jesus rejoicing in the Holy Spirit!) Yet Jesus also warned them to be careful to focus not *on the powerful way that God had used them* but *on the grace of God extended to them* and to the people who had come to know and love God: "Do not rejoice at this, that the spirits submit to you, but rejoice that your names are written in heaven" (10:20). Their focus was to remain on God, his grace, and the authority and power that comes from Jesus.

This narrative recounts events that happened nearly two millennia ago, but it offers guidelines for Christian mission in our own time. It establishes a proper mindset for mission, a right approach to bearing witness, clarity on the message, and the appropriate response to either rejection or acceptance. Today, as the church is beginning to recognize the mission field on its doorstep, this passage offers lessons for leaders seeking to cultivate churches that once again see themselves as sent out to share the gospel.

A Proper Mindset—Trust God

More important than any resource, program, or training in evangelism is the steadfast and joyful belief that God is reconciling the world to himself, one human heart at a time, and that such reconciliation brings new life. Without this core belief, any effort to stir up the church for evangelistic mission will fail. There is no indication that the seventy-two disciples Jesus sent out were particularly gifted evangelists, skilled communicators, or trained apologists. What we do know is that they had come to know Jesus.

There was something about Jesus that was so compelling that, like so many of the people discussed in these biblical conversion stories, they couldn't wait to prepare the way for people to meet him. They knew Jesus in such a way that they trusted him to send them out, and they trusted him to provide the power to heal and witness.

Today we have an abundance of resources and programs aimed at teaching the church how to share the faith. We have slick video series and printed training programs. We have conferences, workshops, and webinars. These can all be useful tools. But without the trust that God's presence and power is real, these tools are useless. Just as the seventy-two disciples were sent out by someone whom they had come to know as authoritative, compassionate, challenging, loving, and life-giving, so too the church in the West must rediscover this person, Jesus of Nazareth. A compelling and life-giving missiology flows from a compelling and life-giving Christology. The church needs to learn how to once again trust in the God who was born and lived among us, taught us, died for us, and was raised to life, all of this a testimony to who he is. His power and knowledge are unfathomable. His righteousness and love are unending.

A Proper Approach to Non-Christians—Build Trust

Jesus instructed his disciples to travel to various communities and to accept the hospitality offered to them. To many of us today this would seem like an odd command, but in the first century it was common to offer hospitality to strangers, and the practice undoubtedly helped build relationships. I wonder what parallels exist today. How can the church learn to go out and build relationships with people who know little to nothing about Christ?

One of the best ways to get to know people is to serve together. Many people of various faiths, or no faith at all, hope to be a force for positive change in their communities. Churches that already offer food pantries and community gardens for the hungry, or Christmas dinners for the lonely, or homework or reading clubs for neighborhood children can make space for people from their community to join them in these efforts. This will take intentional efforts (e.g., advertising, inviting, volunteer screening, orienting, working alongside), but building new relationships always takes effort. Likewise, Christians can look around at good things happening in their communities and join in those efforts as a way to get outside of their walls and intentionally build relationships with their non-Christian neighbors, colleagues, and fellow citizens. This is part of attending to where God is already at work in their communities and joining in that work.

Other activities that can help build relationships involve sharing fun together. Many churches put on a Christmas pageant or go caroling, plan Easter egg hunts, and host Family Day, Canada Day, or Fourth of July events. Why not extend the invitation to others in our communities to join us, intentionally including time for building relationships? On a more ongoing basis, Christians can plan things like a walking or running group, a book club, a knitting group (yes, knitting is back!), or a woodworking club, inviting people on their street to come and get to know one another. New relationships can be the foundation for sharing the faith. Offering and accepting hospitality may not look exactly as it did in the first century, but it is still possible today.

Clarity on the Mission—Be Disciples Who Make Disciples

Jesus's disciples were sent out with a clear mission: to share good news about the kingdom of God, to bring a blessing of peace, and to pray for the healing of those they met. As they did this, people were drawn into the earliest Christian fellowships. They were disciples making disciples, but not in a mechanistic way. This was ministry at its most relational, and it was ministry that resulted in people finding freedom, healing, truth, wholeness, and new life. This was apostolic ministry in that they were sent out with a message of God's kingdom come near (the word "apostle" literally means "messenger").

Clarity on the Message—God Is for Us

At the heart of the gospel is the message that *God is for us*. This is why the Father sent the Son to be born among us, to teach us about God and what it means to be human. *God is for us*. This is why the Son offered up his life, the one sufficient sacrifice for the sins of the whole world. *God is for us*. This is why the Son was raised from the grave, forever disarming the power of sin and death, ushering in the dawn of God's kingdom, and assuring all who turn to him of eternal life. *God is for us*. This is why Jesus sent the Holy Spirit, to comfort, to prod, challenge, remind, and empower the church to serve God in these times. *God is for us*. He is continually calling people back into relationship with himself. He is continually at work in the world that he called into being and loves with an undying love.

Response to Rejection—A Message of Warning and Hope

It is clear from Jesus's commands that the disciples would face some rejection, and it has remained so throughout the ages of the church. Accepting God's love requires people to enter a relationship in which they must acknowledge who God is and who they are to him, and not everyone is ready or willing to do that. But as we've seen in many of these conversion stories, such an acknowledgment often happens in stages. People often awaken gradually to a full understanding of who Jesus is. Someone who rejects the message today may well start the journey toward acceptance tomorrow. The fact that this is a journey did not seem to trouble Jesus at all, and it shouldn't trouble us either. In the face of rejection, Jesus commanded the seventy-two to acknowledge the rejection by issuing a warning but also to leave a final message of hope that the kingdom had come near. Perhaps he knew that the many healings and transformed lives left behind in those communities would continue to witness to the power and presence of God and be the catalyst for other people to become his apprentices.

Response to Ministry Impact—Keep Focused on God's Grace

Even though rejection was clearly possible and almost certainly happened, the seventy-two disciples don't mention it when they report on the impact of the ministry they had performed in Jesus's name. They were excited and inspired by what they had experienced. We know from subsequent verses that Jesus was rejoicing with them for what God had done through them. But he also clearly wanted to protect them from one of the hazards of successful ministry: unhealthy pride. Jesus reminded them that they should instead remain focused on God's grace, which was the source of their own salvation, transformation, and vocation. They were to be grateful, not for the power of their ministry but for their part in extending the grace of God to this broken world.

There are so many church leaders whose ministries have been destroyed because they focused on themselves: their gifts, their status, their success. Jesus's warning to his disciples remains an important reminder to us to stay humble and grateful. Evangelism is ultimately God's work which, amazingly, we are invited to join for the sake of the world God created and loves.

DISCUSSION QUESTIONS

1. What are some things your church currently does that could be tweaked to include those outside the church for the purpose of building relationships with them?
2. Who are the people most in need of healing and a word of hope in your context? What are some possible ways to accept hospitality from such people and to offer them friendship and the good news?
3. Have you known someone who drew nearer to God because you shared the faith with them? Share the impact that experience had on you.

Appendix

Experiments for Your Church to Try

Experiment #1: Invite Some Friends to Dinner Church

Dinner church: A simple Christian gathering that is accessible to seekers, explorers, and the somewhat curious.

Dinner church offers a familiar setting with some already trusted personal connections for people who might be hesitant to attend a more formal expression of church in a church building. It also offers a context of simple hospitality and friendship into which Christians may find it easier to invite their unchurched or dechurched friends, neighbors, and colleagues. Finally, dinner church offers a context in which deeper bonds are encouraged among those attending, as participants share in reading and discussing a passage of Scripture, in praying for and with each other, and in serving in their communities together.

Getting Ready

1. First, pray together for a couple of weeks, asking God to guide your plans and to bless and multiply your efforts

so that new people can come to know Jesus. Agree on a night that will work well for everyone, how often to meet (weekly or biweekly is suggested for the sake of continuity and making deeper connections), and where to meet (usually a home).

2. Then invite others to join in the gathering. Ideally aim for six to ten people, depending on the size of your table, with a mix of Christians and a few people you know well but who are not connected to any faith community. Before you start to invite people, ask God to direct the invitation process. Invitations can be quite personal and informal. For example, an invitation could sound like this:

Shorter version: "I'm getting together with some friends to try something called dinner church. We'll share a meal and talk about a story from one of the early biographies of Jesus. Would you like to come?"

More detailed version: "Some friends and I are trying something called dinner church in which we'll gather for supper and discuss a passage from one of the early biographies of Jesus. Everybody is welcome to bring something to share at the meal. Whether people are already part of a church, have been away for a while, or have no experience at all, we want everyone to feel free to participate as much or as little as they like in the discussion. Would you like to come?"

3. Don't be discouraged if someone declines an invitation to dinner church, especially the first time you ask. Keep the communication path open by saying something like, "No worries. When we get together again, I'll let you know how it went. Maybe next time you'll be able to join."

4. If someone accepts the invitation, ask if they have any food allergies and if they'd like to contribute to the meal. (This can give people a sense of belonging right from the start.) Give them details about location and start and end times to help them plan ahead.

5. As the date approaches, follow up with a phone call or text to let them know you're looking forward to seeing them. Perhaps offer them transportation if appropriate.

6. When getting ready for your first dinner church, remember to keep things simple. This is meant to feel more like a family meal than a formal dinner party. Different opinions and questions are to be expected and encouraged. Hosts and leaders can guide the discussion while also being good listeners, recognizing that some may be just starting their faith journey. When you're not sure how to respond to someone, there's always, "That's an interesting take on things." It lets the person know you appreciate them offering their opinion and so keeps the conversation open without hindering you from offering your own view.

7. If you'd like to try dinner church but worry that some tough questions may be raised about the Scripture passage that you won't be able to answer, relax. This is a discussion between friends. You don't have to answer every question. Just be honest and say something like, "That's a great question . . . and one I have no idea how to answer! But I'll write it down and see if our priest/pastor is able to help us with it."

8. If you have a sense that people would more likely attend an online gathering, an email or phone invitation could look like this:

   "Hey, our church is trying an experiment called dinner church, and I wondered if you might be interested. I'm getting some people together to explore a passage from one of the first biographies of Jesus, but we're doing this online. Would you like to join us for a dinner on Zoom? We plan on looking at one story from Jesus's life and talking about what it might mean in our lives today. I'd love it if you would join in the discussion. I'll have a story chosen, and we'll talk about it together. We might also talk about what's going on in the world and offer up a prayer.

185

I realize that eating in front of one another on Zoom is a bit weird, but some folks are more likely to attend in this format. Would you like to join us?"

Some Suggested Elements to Include as You Meet

1. Gathering and greeting: **everyone brings a contribution for the meal** and gets seated.
2. Dinner is served and **a prayer of thanksgiving** for the food is offered by leader #1 prior to eating.
3. A **Scripture passage** is read aloud by leader #1. Here are a few passages you could choose from:
   - Luke 9:10–17 (Jesus feeds the five thousand)
   - John 4:5–42 (Jesus talks with a Samaritan woman)
   - John 3:1–21 (Jesus talks with Nicodemus, a religious leader)
   - Matthew 22:1–14 (Jesus's parable of the wedding feast)
   - Luke 19:1–10 (Jesus engages Zacchaeus the tax collector)
   - Luke 10:25–37 (Jesus's parable of the good Samaritan)
   - Luke 24:1–12 (the resurrection of Jesus)
4. Food eaten as **discussion** is led by leader #2:
   - What words or phrases stand out for you in the passage?
   - Was anything surprising, confusing, or encouraging?
   - What do you think this passage tells us about Jesus?
   - What are the connections you see between this story and life today?
   - Given what the story teaches about Jesus or the kingdom of God, what do you think this could mean for people learning to follow Jesus?
5. A short **commentary on the Scripture reading** could be read aloud by leader #3 to bring in a thoughtful and scholarly component. This could be from a commentary

series such as N. T. Wright's series For Everyone or even a short reflection written by your pastor/priest.

6. **Members share any challenges they are facing or things they'd like to pray about.** Prayers around the table—or prayers written and placed in a basket to be read aloud. What are the needs of the world and our own lives that we want to bring to God? "God, we lift to you the following needs we see around us and have heard about tonight."

7. Coffee, tea, dessert is shared.

8. People clear their places and assist with cleanup prior to leaving.

9. The **date for the next gathering of dinner church** is mentioned to everyone.

Over time, as participants become more accustomed to dinner church, other elements of Christian worship could be added, fitting these in around the core elements. These include prayers of adoration or thanksgiving to start the meal, reading the Lord's Prayer, the Nicene Creed, or the Ten Commandments together, praying in unison a prayer of confession followed by a proclamation/reminder of God's forgiveness, discussing ways for the group to help meet particular needs in the neighborhood, or reading together the grace (2 Cor. 13:13) to close the mealtime.

What Is the Goal of Dinner Church?

Dinner church can be a vehicle through which Christians offer a simple expression of Christian gathering that allows the curious, explorers, and seekers to learn what Scripture teaches, how Christians pray, and how they serve their communities together. The hope is that dinner church gatherings will grow and multiply as more people join. Once a dinner church reaches ten to twelve people it should split and form two new gatherings.

In many cases, members of a dinner church will also be part of a larger gathering of Christians meeting regularly in a church building for worship. In communities that don't have a church building, or where the building is no longer in regular use, dinner church may become the primary form of Christian meeting, with larger gatherings happening less frequently. Such dinner church gatherings function more like cell churches, where cell church lay leaders are equipped by the clergy to lead their cell. In such settings pastors/priests may travel from cell to cell to lead sacramental ministry (in denominations requiring this) and to continue to encourage and support the leaders of each dinner church.

Experiment #2: Invite a Friend to Have Three Conversations about Stories from the Original Biographies of Jesus

Gospel conversations: conversations that make stories from the Gospels accessible to seekers, explorers, and the somewhat curious.

Having a conversation over a cup of coffee or tea is a familiar way for people to meet with friends or colleagues. For people who might be hesitant to attend a formal expression of church, a simple conversation can allow them to talk about their own perceptions of Jesus, to learn more about him for themselves, and to voice their own spiritual questions and longings. These personal conversations also offer a context of simple hospitality and friendship to which Christians may find it easier to invite their unchurched or dechurched friends, neighbors, and colleagues. While the data suggests fewer people are going to church, it also indicates that many believe in God, pray regularly, and have spiritual questions they can't readily discuss with anyone.[1] In such an age, it is critical to equip all Christians to be transmitters of the gospel message. For that to happen, we will all need to engage with the people around us in a context in which they are comfortable. A conversation over coffee may be a simple yet profound way in which someone you know begins to consider the person of Jesus for themselves.

1. Ray Pennings and Jenisa Los, "The Shifting Landscape of Faith in Canada," Cardus, 2022, https://www.cardus.ca/research/spirited-citizenship/reports/the-shifting-landscape-of-faith-in-canada.

Tips for Gospel Conversations

1. **Begin with prayer.**

   - Ask God to bring someone to mind in your life who doesn't have any church connection. This could be a family member, friend, neighbor, colleague, or even a new acquaintance. They might be someone who once was part of a church but drifted away or someone who has never been connected to a church.

   - Ask God to give you an opportunity and the right words as you invite them to have these conversations.

2. Try this experiment with others in your church so you can pray for each other as you have these conversations with unchurched and dechurched people.

3. **Invite.** Here are some examples of invitations:

   "Our church is hoping to learn to talk with people beyond our congregation about spiritual issues. Would you be interested in meeting with me a few times over coffee to explore some passages from the earliest biographies of Jesus?"

   "Our church is trying something called Gospel Conversations, where we meet over coffee with a friend or neighbor to discuss three different stories from the life of Jesus. I'd love to hear your views on these encounters people had with Jesus. Would you be interested?"

   "Along with others in my church, I'm trying to learn how to talk with other people in my life about questions of faith. Would you be interested in meeting over coffee a few times to discuss some passages taken from the Bible about the life of Jesus?"

   If you think a small group discussion would be less threatening than a one-on-one conversation, you might invite a couple of friends. Perhaps these are people who share a hobby with you or are members of a group that you belong to. For such people you could use this sort of invite:

189

"Would you be interested in joining a small discussion group that explores some of the stories from Jesus's life found in the Bible? My plan is pretty low-key: just to meet for coffee and chat together, meeting two or three times. What do you think?"

4. **Pray again . . . as you select three passages** to discuss together in your Gospel conversations. What passages might resonate with the person you will meet with? Here are some examples to choose from:

- John 4:5–42 (Jesus talks with a woman at a well)
- John 3:1–21 (Jesus talks with Nicodemus, a religious leader)
- Luke 19:1–10 (Jesus engages Zacchaeus, a tax collector for the Roman Empire)
- Luke 10:25–37 (Jesus's parable of the good Samaritan)
- Luke 24:1–12 (the resurrection of Jesus)

5. **During the conversations, let the following questions be a guide,** but don't feel bound to them. Ask the Holy Spirit to guide the conversation.

- What words or phrases stand out for you?
- What do you think this passage tells us about the culture of the day?
- What do you think this passage wants us to know about Jesus?
- Do you see any connection with our lives today?

6. **Don't worry if they have questions that you don't know how to respond to.** Simply admit that, and let them know that you'll ask someone who might be able to address what they've raised. Perhaps that will be your pastor or another member of your church. Remember, this is a conversation, and conversations are different from a Q and A session.

7. **Be ready to suggest a possible next step** if they seem interested in further exploring questions about Jesus,

Christianity, and faith in general. Are you willing to keep meeting? Is there a book you could read together and discuss? Would they like to meet over coffee with you and your pastor? Would they like you to pray for them? Test these waters gingerly, but don't be shy to encourage them to keep exploring.

8. **Enjoy your conversations!** Be open to where God may take these conversations. Perhaps you will have simply planted a seed that will germinate much later. Perhaps you'll meet regularly. Perhaps you'll invite them to dinner church or a book club or some other easy-access event or program at your church. Above all be genuine and love them as Jesus would have you love them.

Experiment #3: Invite a Friend or Colleague to Join You in Exploring the Claims of Christianity

Most Christians affirm that it's important for their church to share the faith. But many also think *someone else* is better suited to that task than they are. Here are some common perspectives on evangelism found in the church:

- Evangelism is the job of pastors, who have theological training.
- It is best done by especially gifted communicators known as "evangelists."
- It requires someone who has great answers to tough philosophical questions.
- It can only be done by someone who knows the Bible far better than I do.
- It must be done by people whose lives are holier than my own life.

But what if we believed that God is already calling people all around us back into relationship with himself and that we are all

191

called to participate in that work of reconciliation? What would happen if all Christians everywhere believed that, just as they are, they could be used by God to help someone take steps toward him?

Plenty of data indicates that there are many people with spiritual questions and longings who would be open to exploring faith issues if they were invited by a friend to do so.[2] Sometimes labeled "privately faithful," this group is made up of people who have no connection to any faith community, but they report believing in God, praying to God, and wanting their children to learn about the faith. If we cared about reaching such people, how might we do it?

This experiment is something churches can work on together. They can offer several evenings geared specifically to helping explorers and seekers address their spiritual questions and longings. Church members would invite people in their lives who have no connection to a faith community to attend these evenings with them. That last bit is key. People are more likely to attend an event offered by a church, or in the home of a church member, if they personally know someone there.

There is a wealth of free or inexpensive resources that churches can use. Here are six that we recommend:

1. Christianity Explored, www.christianityexplored.org

   This ten-session course, developed in the UK, uses a series of videos to help people engage with Scripture so they can explore such questions as: Who is Jesus? Why did he come? Why did Jesus die? What is grace? What was his resurrection about? What is a Christian?

   This website also provides a series of short videos that address some of the most difficult questions people pose about the existence of God, suffering, evil and good, religion, and what God has to do with our life today. A discussion group focused on these short videos could be another great way to spark conversation that addresses

---

2. Pennings and Los, "Shifting Landscape of Faith in Canada."

people's questions: www.christianityexplored.org/what-is
-christianity/tough-questions.

2. Nua, https://nuafilmseries.org

Nua, which means "new" in Irish, is a series of short
films produced by Scripture Union Ireland. These fifteen-
minute, free downloadable films address such questions as,
How did we get here? Jesus: fact or fiction? What about
the resurrection? What was Jesus really like? Why do I
like Jesus but struggle with Christians? How can you say
that God is good? Has the church caused more harm than
good? What's Jesus got to do with me?

3. Jesus the Game Changer, www.olivetreemedia.com.au
/jesus-the-game-changer

This ten-part documentary series, produced by Olive
Tree Media in Australia, explores how the life and teachings of Jesus changed the world and why it matters. Each
film touches on how Jesus changed the way the world
viewed such issues as equality, forgiveness, women and
children, democracy, care, leadership, health, wealth, and
science. Footage from all over the world is included as sci-
entists, theologians, political leaders, financial leaders, his-
torians, and biblical scholars from many different cultures
are interviewed.

4. The Alpha Course, https://alphausa.org, https://alpha
canada.org

Whether you live in North America, Europe, the UK,
New Zealand, Australia, or many other countries, you can
freely download the Alpha Course.

This popular and helpful course aims at helping people
explore Christianity. The fifteen video sessions (three of
which are usually run as part of a weekend retreat focused
on the person and work of the Holy Spirit) allow people
to address such questions as, Is there more to life than
this? Who is Jesus? Why did he die? How can I have faith?
How and why should I pray? How and why should I read

the Bible? How does God guide us? How can I make the most of the rest of my life? How can I resist evil? Why and how should I tell others? Does God heal today? What about the church?

5. Christian Foundations, www.wycliffecollege.ca/christian -foundations

Unlike the courses profiled above, this resource is not a film series. Instead, it uses a workbook format that includes short narratives followed by discussion questions and a variety of interactive exercises to help people explore such questions as, How can I know and serve God? What is the story of Israel? Who is Jesus? What do Christians believe? Why are there so many sorts of Christians? How can I grow in my faith? What is my part in the kingdom of God?

Some churches have used these workbooks as a baptism preparation program, as a resource preparing teens or adults for confirmation, as a small group resource to better ground Christians in the faith, or as a tool for one-on-one discipleship.

6. Being With, https://being-with.org/being-with-one.

This ten-session course emphasizes the role of community in people's exploration of the faith. It invites people to discover faith in the context of discovering friendship, placing belonging before believing.

BIBLIOGRAPHY

Anglican Church of Canada. *The Book of Alternative Services.* Toronto: Anglican Book Center, 1985.

Anglican Church of Canada. *The Book of Common Prayer.* Toronto: Anglican Book Center, 1962.

Balz, Horst, and Gerhard Schneider, eds. *Exegetical Dictionary of the New Testament*, vol. 2. Grand Rapids: Eerdmans, 1991.

Bosch, David J. "The Structure of Mission: An Exposition of Matthew 28:16–21." In *The Study of Evangelism*, edited by Paul Chilcote and Laceye Warner, 73–92. Grand Rapids: Eerdmans, 2008.

Doyle, Tom, and Greg Webster. *Dreams and Visions: Is Jesus Awakening the Muslim World?* Nashville: Thomas Nelson, 2012.

Everts, Don, and Doug Schaupp. *I Once Was Lost: What Postmodern Skeptics Taught Us about Their Path to Jesus.* Downers Grove, IL: InterVarsity, 2008.

Everts, Don, Doug Schaupp, and Val Gordon. *Breaking the Huddle: How Your Community Can Grow Its Witness.* Downers Grove, IL: InterVarsity, 2016.

Groome, Thomas H. *Sharing Faith: The Way of Shared Praxis.* New York: HarperCollins, 1991.

Guder, Darrell L. "Incarnation and the Church's Evangelistic Mission." In *The Study of Evangelism*, edited by Paul Chilcote and Laceye Warner, 171–84. Grand Rapids: Eerdmans, 2008.

Hunter, George G., III. *The Celtic Way of Evangelism: How Christianity Can Reach the West Again*. Nashville: Abingdon, 2000.

InterVarsity Christian Fellowship. "The Five Thresholds." Twentyonehundred Publications. https://vimeo.com/showcase/3605316.

Keener, Craig. *Acts: An Exegetical Commentary*. 4 vols. Grand Rapids: Baker Academic, 2012–2015.

Lehane, Brendan. *The Quest of Three Abbots: The Golden Age of Celtic Christianity*. New York: Viking, 1968.

Marshall, I. Howard. *The Gospel of Luke*. New International Greek Testament Commentary. Grand Rapids: Eerdmans, 1995.

Mercadante, Linda A. *Belief without Borders: Inside the Minds of the Spiritual but Not Religious*. New York: Oxford University Press, 2014.

Newbigin, Lesslie. *The Gospel in a Pluralist Society*. Grand Rapids: Eerdmans, 1989.

Reese, Martha Grace. *Unbinding the Gospel: Real Life Evangelism*. St. Louis: Chalice, 2007.

Stackhouse, John G. *Humble Apologetics: Defending the Faith Today*. Oxford: Oxford University Press, 2002.

Stone, Bryan. *Evangelism after Christendom: The Theology and Practice of Christian Witness*. Grand Rapids: Brazos, 2008.

———. *Finding Faith Today*. Eugene, OR: Cascade Books, 2018.

Stott, John R. "The Great Commission." In *One Race, One Gospel, One Task*, vol. 1, edited by Carl F. Henry and W. W. Mooneyhan. Minneapolis: World Wide Publications, 1967.

Talman, Harley, and John Jay Travis, eds. *Understanding Insider Movements: Disciples of Jesus within Diverse Religious Communities*. Pasadena, CA: William Carey Library, 2015.

Vaughn, J. Patrick. "Evangelism: A Pastoral Theological Perspective." In *The Study of Evangelism*, edited by Paul Chilcote and Laceye Warner, 264–74. Grand Rapids: Eerdmans, 2008.

Walton, John, Victor Matthews, and Mark Chavalas. *IVP Bible Background Commentary—Old Testament*. Downers Grove, IL: InterVarsity, 2000.

Wright, N. T. *Luke for Everyone*. Louisville: John Knox, 2004.

SCRIPTURE INDEX

197

198

SUBJECT INDEX

201

ecclesial practices, 86–92, 117, 146
elders, 109
Eli, 101, 103, 105–6
Elisha, 67–68, 69, 71, 74–75, 76–77
Elkanah, 103, 105, 106, 108
Enquiry into the Obligations of Christians to Use Means for the Conversion of the Heathens, An (Carey), 164
Ethiopian eunuch, conversion of, 29–30
  baptism and, 30, 39–40
  Holy Spirit and, 29–30, 38
  listening and, 36, 37
  outsider status and, 32–34, 35, 37
  preexisting spiritual life and, 30, 38
  significance for gentiles, 62n4
eunuchs, 32–33
evangelism. *See also* witness
  accepting hospitality and, 134
  audience awareness in, 123–24
  avoidance of, 3–4
  building trust in, 19, 177–79
  call for response in, 39–40, 123, 145, 151
  children's growth and, 107–8
  Christocentric, 38–39, 133, 150–51, 168–69
  by church, 80–81, 88–89, 93–95
  context for, 114, 116–17, 119, 144–45
  conversion stories in, 124–25
  crossing cultural boundaries in, 63, 168
  cultural bridges in, 47–48, 57–58
  cultural references in, 149–50
  ecclesial practices and. *See* ecclesial practices
  faith and, 74
  fasting and, 21
  friendship, 7
  gardening metaphor for, 18–24
  God's primacy in, 17, 30, 59–60, 171–72
  Great Commission and, 163–65
  Holy Spirit's role in, 21, 30, 38, 55

Jesus's approach to, 123, 167–69, 181
  knowledge of gospel in, 125–26
  listening in. *See* listening
  love and, 35–37, 93–94, 170–71
  making disciples and, 179
  message in, 80, 180
  models of, 49, 50, 93–95, 164–65
  motives and warrants for, 35–36, 69, 77–83, 126, 170–71
  by multiple people, 69, 74–75
  negative attitudes about, 3, 4–10
  obedience and, 61–62, 164–65
  by ordinary Christians, 73–74, 75–76
  by parents, 108–9
  personal experience in, 124–25, 144–45
  prayer and, 21, 36, 59, 95–96, 124, 133
  preexisting spiritual lives and, 46–48, 56–58
  rejection of Jesus and, 160, 180
  relationships and, 44–46, 134
  Scripture compelling in, 38
  spiritual growth and, 62–65
  suffering acknowledged in, 34, 40, 154–55
  trusting God in, 177–78
Evangelism after Christendom (Stone), 93
evangelistic preaching
  hallmarks of, 149–52
  importance of, 146–47
  occasions for, 147–48
  of Peter, 55, 60, 139–46
evangelistic teaching, 133, 134–35
evangelists, 8, 31, 73–74
Eve, 82
Everts, Don, 19, 20, 22, 23
evil, 156, 157–58
experience, personal, 124–25, 144–45

faith, 74
families
  engaging with unchurched, 110–11
  known by God, 103
fasting, 21

fear, 155, 156, 158, 160
Festus, 121, 122
freedom of religion, 96
Fresh Expressions, 97–98
friendship evangelism, 7

gathering together, 87–88
Gehazi, 68, 69, 72, 77
genti Gerasene demoniac, conversion
    of, 153–54
les, conversion of, 62, 62n4, 64, 65
    effects of evil and, 156, 157–58
    fearful response to, 156, 158, 160
    suffering and, 155, 158
    witness after, 156, 160–61
God
    Abraham blessed by, 50, 78
    alienation from, 81
    brokenness addressed by, 72–73
    character/nature of, 79–80
    children and, 102, 109–10
    conversion as work of, 16–17, 38,
        58–59, 142
    "for us," 180
    grace of, 38, 58–59, 181
    love for, 35–36
    metanarrative of, 106
    mission of, 49, 78, 79, 81, 111–12, 179
    mystical instruments of, 60–61
    as primary Evangelist, 17, 30, 59–60,
        171–72
    relationship to families, 103
    relationship to individuals, 38, 64,
        103–4
    shalom of, 73
gospel
    as good news, 34–35, 146, 180
    meta- and micronarratives in, 124–26
    suffering for, 96–97
    syncretization of, 63
grace, 38, 58–59, 181
Graham, Billy, 5n8, 8
grandparents, 108–9
Great Commission, 163–65. *See also*
    evangelism

Groome, Thomas, 11
Guder, Darrell, 93
guilt, 8–9

Hadad (Syrian god), 76
Hannah, 103, 105, 106, 108
Herod Agrippa II, 122
Holy Spirit
    in Acts narratives, 130
    outpouring of, 60, 139, 140, 142
    role in conversion, 29–30, 38, 55, 60,
        141–42
    role in evangelism, 21, 30, 37
Hophni, 103, 105
hospitality, 134
households, conversion and baptism of,
    62, 65–66, 92, 98, 129, 132
Humble Apologetics (Stackhouse), 6
Hunter, George, 47, 49, 50, 94–95

identity, 24, 25, 63–64
incarnational model of evangelism,
    93–94, 165
individualism, 65, 135–36
injustice, systemic, 99
insider movements, 63–64
I Once Was Lost (Everts, Schaupp), 19
Israel, 103

jailer. *See* prison warden, conversion of
Jesus
    confidence in, 10
    disciples' relationships with, 45–46
    disciples sent by, 78–79, 134, 174–81
    evangelism of, 123, 167–69, 181
    focusing on, 38–39, 133, 150–51
    interaction with outcasts, 14, 17,
        153–54, 155–56, 158–60, 165–69
    rejection of, 160, 180
    specific audiences addressed by, 123
    on suffering, 90
    suffering and persecution of, 34–35,
        36, 115, 117
    unafraid of evil, 158

slave girl, 67, 70, 71, 73–74, 75
sphere of influence, 73–74, 75–76
spiritual disciplines, 36, 152. *See also*
    prayer
spiritual formation, 50–51
spiritual lives, preexisting, 30, 38,
    46–48, 56–58, 131
Stackhouse, John, 6
Stephen, 113–14
Stone, Bryan, 93
Stott, John, 164
suffering. *See also* brokenness
    awareness/understanding of, 40
    Christian community and, 89–90, 117
    evangelism and, 34, 40, 154–55
    of Gerasene demoniac, 155, 158
    for gospel, 96–97
    of Jesus, 34–35, 36
    of Naaman, 67, 70
    as normative in early church, 89–90,
        117
    of Paul and Silas, 89, 99, 117

teaching, evangelistic, 133, 134–35
theology, 79–80
Theophilus, 116
Timothy, 89, 129, 130, 131, 135
traveling together, 87–88
trust, 19, 177–79

unchurched people
    acknowledging doubts of, 19–20, 149
    building trust with, 178–79

cultural bridges with, 47–48, 57–58
engaging with families, 110–11
evangelistic preaching for, 147–52
listening to, 34, 37–38, 143–44, 145, 150
love for, 36–37
preexisting spiritual lives of, 30, 38,
    46–48, 56–58, 131
prevenient grace and, 38, 58–59
spiritual categories for, 108n2, 110,
    188, 192
United States, 9–10
Ursinus, Johann, 164

Vaughn, J. Patrick, 154
visions, 60–61. *See also specific stories*
vocation, 104, 106, 111–12

Welz, Justinian von, 164
Wesley, John, 58
witness. *See also* evangelism
    baptism as, 65–66, 92, 98
    of changed life, 20, 156, 160–61
    of church, 88–89, 93–95
    of Gerasene demoniac, 159, 160–61
    in metanarrative of God, 106
    of Samaritan woman, 169
    vocation and, 104, 106
    of words and deeds, 21
    worship as, 97–98
worship, 18, 24, 90–91, 97–98
Wright, N. T., 155
Wycliffe College, 1n1